The Edo period and Japan's fables provide a model for a sustainable Japan

The Edo period and Japan's fables provide a model for a sustainable

Cheryl Lans

February 9 2013

ISBN 978-0-9880852-3-7

Table

The Project Gutenberg EBook of Japanese Fairy Tales, by Yei Theodora Ozaki
THE TONGUE-CUT SPARROW
THE ADVENTURES OF KINTARO, THE GOLDEN BOY.
THE BAMBOO-CUTTER AND THE MOON-CHILD.
THE MIRROR OF MATSUYAMA A STORY OF OLD JAPAN
MOMOTARO, OR THE STORY OF THE SON OF A PEACH.
THE WHITE HARE AND THE CROCODILES
Yuki-onna by Lafcadio Hearn (Koizumi Yakumo) from Kwaidan (1904)

The Edo period and Japan's fables provide a model for a sustainable Japan

Essay

For a long time many developing countries have focused on increasing productivity and less time debating the question of what constitutes the good society. Japan's Edo period constituted the good society; it was very innovative and self-sustaining. While the essay topic indicates some distress about Japan's shrinking population, many traditional folk tales of Japan such as *'The Tongue-Cut Sparrow'*, *'The Farmer and The Badger'*, *'The Adventures of Kintaro, the Golden Boy'*, *'The Bamboo-Cutter and the Moon-Child'*, *'The Mirror of Matsuyama'* and several others describe parents with one or no children.

While some of these parents were disappointed with their fate, they all lived interesting lives that are still transmitted from generation to generation. One of the few mothers with many children was the evil Yuki-onna who remained beautiful in middle age because she was not human[i]. I commend Japan for their decreasing population because the earth's carrying capacity was probably exceeded more than six years ago. Japan's land area is slightly smaller than the state of California and its population density is 836 per square mile, far higher than Canada at 9, Sweden at 57, France at 289 and even Haiti at 781[ii]. This high density is reflected in the need for order, *oshiyas* and the focus on miniaturization as in the cultural traditions of *bonsai* and sushi making and technology such as calculators, compact discs, cameras and compact cars. The population during the Edo period was 30 million and Japan was self-sufficient during that time; very little was imported[iii]. Currently Japan imports 78% of its energy, 60% of its food[iv] and 82% of its timber for construction[v]. The Edo period was a very creative period in Japan and included the development of the mechanized dolls[vi] that became the robots of today. A smaller population can therefore be an aid to innovation.

The population of Japan reached the replacement level in the 1970s and peaked at 127.79 million people in 2004. Japan then had the world's tenth largest population. Life expectancy has increased from 76.9 in 1980 to 82.6 currently (see Raines, 2007). The share of people over 65 in Japan in 2006 was 20.6% and is expected to increase to 28.7% in 2025 and to 35.7% by 2050[vii]. Japan has always prided itself on how long its elders live, so having an aging population should not be a cultural shock or a problem for the Japanese. Other countries such as Italy, South Korea, Singapore, Hong Kong and China also have decreasing populations and I hope that they can serve as an example for many African countries.

Figure 1. Poverty levels in Japan. Source: Iwata and Nishizawa, 2008.

Japan does not need to fear that it will be overwhelmed culturally or militarily if neighboring countries also have decreasing populations. Other countries would also feel more secure if there was no country exempting itself from planetary constraints. The birthrate for Japanese women in 2005 was 1.26 children[viii]. A decline of 0.2 percent in the population to 127.8 million can hardly be described as drastic[ix]. The decline of the population may have had a negative effect on economic growth. But unlike the environment, the economic programs and the welfare programs are human constructions and can be changed to match the decline in the population. For example, the long-term employment and seniority-based compensation traditional to Japanese companies changed in the past decade[x] to match changes in the economy. It did not follow timeless patterns like the seasonal migration of birds. This decrease in employer-employee loyalty resulted in a higher than traditional unemployment rate and increased poverty (see Figure 1. Poverty Levels in Japan[xi]).

Population reduction was planned since the 1950s by men such as John D. Rockefeller who set up the Population Council and met with or shared the views of the International Planned Parenthood Federation (IPPF), William Vogt of the Planned Parenthood Federation of America (PPFA), Paul Ehrlich, Julian Huxley of UNESCO, the UN, the World Bank, pharmaceutical firms, and the Ford Foundation[xii]. These international agencies thought it would be useful to plan for tomorrow even if the mice in the ceiling laughed at their plans. Their motives were probably not pure[xiii] and perhaps they were motivated by a need for Western countries to control natural resources, but the underlying fact that natural resources are limited remains unchanged.

Forgetting that population decline was in fact planned for, this decline in combination with an aging society has been linked by some researchers to inappropriate gender norms[xiv]. Kim (2009) refers to the conservative Confucian society as one of the factors influencing gender inequality. In 1972 a large majority of women thought that they should stay home and raise children while their husbands worked outside the home[xv]. In 2002, only 43.2 % of women agreed with these traditional gender roles. However, if a woman leaves the workforce before age 30 and does not return until age 42 or older, her career options are limited.

Italy and Spain are conservative Catholic countries and the situation there is similar; women are considered to be the primary homemakers and childcare is not as available as in France where there is an increasing emphasis on state-provided childcare and parental leave. Care of children does not need to be a twenty-four hour, seven-day-a-week job. It should be possible for more childcare or for early-age schooling to be made available so that women could work part-time. Women can either work for a few hours a day; or it may be more convenient for women to work for eight hours, two or three days a week. This would be a committed three-day work-week until the child goes to a regular school on a full time basis, not a *mikka bouzu*. This will help women succeed in careers where large companies want their employees to have skills that are specific to their company (Yoshimura and Anderson, 1997). This would have to be a nationwide plan so that career-women will not be criticized as *Deru kui wa utareru*. Children are more easily socialized in groups and they could learn traditional games and culture while they are away from their mothers.

"If you think in terms of a year, plant a seed;
if in terms of ten years, plant trees;
if in terms of 100 years, teach the people."
-Confucius

In one version of the folk tale 'The Adventures of Kintaro, the Golden Boy'[xvi], Kintaro's mother Yama-uba lived in the Ashigara Mountains. Providing for him in that situation would have been a full-time job. She did not have to care for her parents but Kintaro did care for her when he was Chief and she was aged. Child and elder care could be combined at special facilities since old people love to tell stories, especially about their own childhoods. Older children could form apprenticeship relationships with these older adults and engage in hands-on activities that pass on cultural traditions or indigenous knowledge.

Indigenous knowledge is local, orally-transmitted knowledge which is often obtained from practical experimentation, repeated use and experience, and it is transferred from generation to generation through stories. For example in the story of the 'White Hare and the Crocodiles'[xvii], a hare played a trick on some crocodiles in order to cross to the mainland of Inaba. When he jeered at them and told them he had played a trick on them, they pulled out his fur. A kind-hearted prince advised the hare to roll in kaba flowers because the pollen would help his fur grow back, and it would alleviate his pain. Assuming that kaba is the Japanese name for birch; birch pollen commonly causes allergies in humans and would provoke an immune response. Birch pollen can be a source of methyl salicylate[xviii]. Methyl salicyate is produced by many plants and it is used by humans to treat pain. Perhaps future research could investigate whether birch pollen could provide a cure for male-pattern baldness. Indigenous knowledge related to animal health is often a source of new drug development and research into traditional practices is usually conducted to assess its usefulness.

I hear and I forget. I see and I remember. I do and I understand.
- Confucius

The Edo period and Japan's fables provide a model for a sustainable Japan

Apparently Japan has already existing, but underused public buildings, museums and concert halls that could be used in the provision of this educational and cultural training (Hay, 2009). Adults coming into these care facility on a daily basis can be separated into adult-only or intergenerational activities according to their health or mood[xix]. Video games and other technology could be improved to be used in these child/elder care facilities. Since the invention of television there have been concerns about the effect of this technology on the eyes[xx]; is it really just a case of needing to blink more, in order to alleviate the negative effects of staring at the screen for long periods ? There were also concerns that this type of technology forces viewers to sit for too long resulting in reduced fitness. Some of those concerns have been addressed with the Nintendo Wii game technology.

Modern gender roles were depicted in the 1994 Taiwanese film *Yinshi nannu*, the English title is *Eat Drink Man Woman*, directed by Ang Lee. Chef Chu is the primary caregiver for his three adult daughters and since he is semi-retired he has time to court a younger woman, so his oldest daughter will not have to care for him. His skills as a father helped him attract his young wife when it was expected that he might settle down with her mother. The secret to his successful life is that he is perfectly matched[xxi] to his job at the Taipei Grand Hotel. Additionally it is a high-quality job rewarding innovation, skills and excellence. With a smaller population it is easier to have this kind of employment match. A larger population in theory gives employers far more choice. In practice however, employers do not want to read through hundreds of applications whenever they are hiring. Chef Chu was also respected for his long-years of experience. Chef Chu did not talk much about age discrimination but he does retire early rather than die on the job. Some women experience age discrimination when they try to return to work after raising children.

> *"To put the world in order, we must first put the nation in order;*
> *to put the nation in order, we must put the family in order;*
> *to put the family in order, we must cultivate our personal life;*
> *and to cultivate our personal life, we must first set our hearts right."*
> -Confucius

Starting school early and attending pre-school programs part-time while their mothers worked; combined with a smaller population would also serve as a dual-pronged approach to remove some of the pressure from women to prepare their children for college. Some of the additional schooling could be used as preparation time and fewer children means less competition. Salaries for women working in early childhood education should be increased because the early years are very important in the education of children.

This means the Japanese government should pay for childcare or early childhood education and remove the incentives for companies to encourage men to work long hours and to not take parental leave. Men on parental leave may have time to think up new technologies that could reinvigorate the Japanese economy. For example the food value of instant noodles could be improved with legumes, barley and oat bran; with seaweeds and herbs in the soup base. University students and poor people all over the world consume these noodles because of budgetary constraints. If their nutritional quality could be improved without raising the price too much this would make an immense if humble contribution to mankind. Alternatively men may have the time to identify indigenous institutions or processes that could be renewed using modern techniques. Or they may have time to research culturally appropriate medicines that could lead to healthy aging. Men grown accustomed to construction projects funded by government could build sand castles or wooden toys with their children.

Having this type of focus for the economy means that if the local government has state funds that need to be spent before the end of the fiscal year, these funds should be spent on elder and childcare if the infrastructure in the locality is in reasonably good condition[xxii]. The proportion of children who do not support their aged parents leaving them dependent on the government is said to be only 0.4% of all welfare payments[xxiii] (see Figure 2).

Growing Dependent
Recipients of welfare payments in Japan, in millions

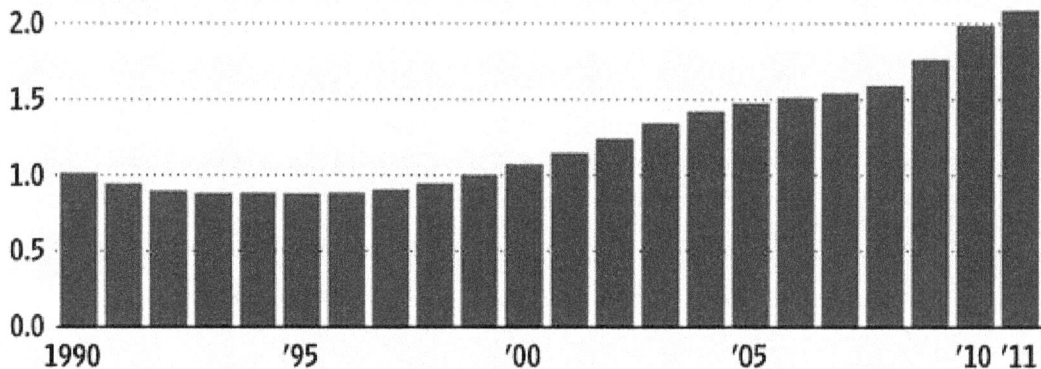

Source: Ministry of Health, Labor and Welfar   The Wall Street Journal

Figure 2. Growing Dependent. Recipients of welfare payments in Japan, in millions. Source: Hyashi, 2012.

A 1998 report by the Japan Institute for Local Government, found that for every 1 trillion yen, or about $11.2 billion, spent on social services like care for the elderly and monthly pension payments, a multiplier effect was achieved providing 1.64 trillion yen in growth (Fackler, 2009). Financing for schools and education provided a stimulative effect of 1.74 trillion yen; greater than the 1.37 trillion yen generated by infrastructure projects. Japan spent $2.1 trillion on public works from 1991 to 1995 and is said to spend $208 billion a year on public work projects or 40% of the national budget[xxivxxv]. Professor Toshihiro Ihori of the University of Tokyo told the New York Times that too much of the stimulus money was spent on construction projects in rural areas and it made community members dependent on construction spending for employment which disappeared at the end of the project. An overreliance on large-scale construction projects did not stimulate the economy as much as was anticipated.

The Edo period and Japan's fables provide a model for a sustainable Japan

"In hindsight, Japan should have built public works that address the problems it faces today, like aging, energy and food sources," said Takehiko Hobo, a Professor Emeritus of public finance at Shimane University in Matsue, Shimane. "This obsession with building roads is a holdover from an earlier era." (Fackler, 2009)

Now that the infrastructure is there however, Japan can try to become the academic conference centre of the future to make good use of its airports, so that the investment is not wasted. It can also host fairs or conferences to show off its *chindōgu*. Even though these are fun inventions having them publicized may lead someone to modify them to make them more useful. The development of sustainable technology involves learning, participation and discussion. Farmers and inventors are not on the receiving end of knowledge produced by scientists, but are active creators. These creations are often easily adopted by others. Some traditional technology like straw mats and modified *chindōgu* may be useful in African refugee camps. These camps could also utilize technology such as solar cookers and other technology for small spaces that the Japanese have perfected over centuries. For a refugee some of this technology may seem like a miracle - like a duck walking towards them carrying its own leeks for its own cooking. Providing small-scale technology instead of money would also reduce unemployment in Japan.

Having hosted the Summer and Winter Olympic Games in Tokyo (1964), Sapparo (1972) and Nagano (1998), and several FIFA Club World Cup competitions (2005, 2006, 2007, 2008, 2011, 2012) and the 2012 under-20 women's World Cup; Japan can continue to host large and small athletic and sporting events to make use of their existing infrastructure.

The future Japanese economy can be imagined by reinterpreting the *Senryū Nakanunara, koroshiteshimae, hototogisu* (If the cuckoo does not sing, kill it).

There are some instances where workers are depicted dying on the job while working for hierarchical companies that do not provide high-quality jobs. The Japanese government spent 4% of its budget in 2012 on basic welfare payments – the livelihood system (Hayashi, 2012). The aging consumer is said to be buying little but it is also the case that poorly paid or unemployed young workers could purchase goods to stimulate the Japanese economy if they were paid better. Japanese companies invested $34 billion in foreign companies to keep themselves solvent during the downturn. This is an indication that the many construction projects undertaken since the 1990s by successive Japanese governments did not stimulate the economy in a self-sustaining way (Inagaki and Fukase 2012)[xxvi].

Thomas A. Kochan, Bunker professor of management, MIT's Sloan School of Management, and co-director of the MIT Institute for Work and Employment Research was interviewed in the Fall issue of Harvard Magazine[xxvii]. He decried persistent high unemployment in the US economy in words that also have relevance for the current Japanese economy:

"30 years of stagnating wages and growing wage inequality, two decades of declining job satisfaction and loss of pension and retirement benefits... and the consequences of unemployment on family life. If we really valued work and human resources, we would address these problems with the vigor required to solve them"...

"The root cause is that motivation—to get short-term shareholder returns—then pushes to lower priority all the other things we used to think about as a social contract: that wages and productivity should go together, that there should be an alignment between the interest of American business and the overall American economy and society. That creates a *market* failure: it's not in the interest of an *individual* firm to address all of the consequences of unemployment and loss of high-quality jobs, but the business community overall depends on high-quality jobs to produce the purchasing power needed to sell their goods and services to the American market. Sixty percent of U.S.-based multinational corporations' revenue still comes from the U.S. market. We've got to solve this market failure".... our business schools particularly have receded into the same myopic view of the economic system where finance rules everything, so we aren't training the next generation of leaders to manage businesses in ways that work for both investors and shareholders and for employees in the community."

Former FDIC Chairman Sheila Bair made similar comments to those of Kochan's in the introduction that she wrote for the book written by Yalman Onaran[xxviii] '*Zombie Banks: How Broken Banks And Debtor Nations Are Crippling the Global Economy* '. "Ironically, the political debate over how to restart the global economy is devoid of any acknowledgement of the role a bloated financial services industry plays in impeding growth,".... "Until government policymakers come to grips with the basic economic truths reflected in this book, our road to recovery will be a very slow and costly one."

Nakanunara, nakashitemiseyou, hototogisu (If the cuckoo does not sing, coax it).

A future economy for Japan should have a more egalitarian relationship between companies and their workforce. Companies should value individual talents, provide high-quality work and allow for more family time for both men and women.

Bongaarts (2004) authored a report on population aging and the effect of this on pensions.[xxix]

He presented several options, only one of which I agree with – increased labor force participation. His other solutions, which are often seen in the US and UK media, are to encourage higher fertility, permit more immigration, raise the age at retirement and reduce public pension benefits. My preferred solution is a higher tax on profitable firms and banks. The combined net profits of Mitsubishi UFJ Financial Group Inc., Sumitomo Mitsui Financial Group Inc., and Mizuho Financial Group Inc. totaled $25 billion[xxx]. The government should be able to recover some of this profit to supplement pensions, especially since the government has traditionally supported the growth of Japanese companies and spent a lot of taxpayer money reviving the banking sector[xxxi].

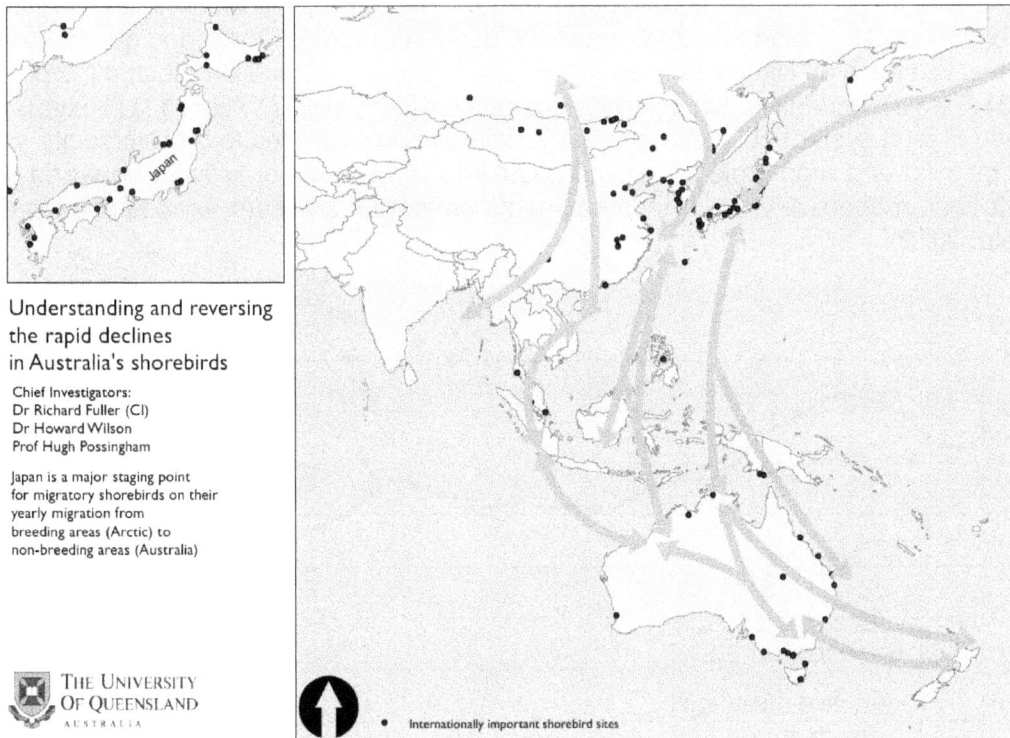

Understanding and reversing the rapid declines in Australia's shorebirds

Chief Investigators:
Dr Richard Fuller (CI)
Dr Howard Wilson
Prof Hugh Possingham

Japan is a major staging point for migratory shorebirds on their yearly migration from breeding areas (Arctic) to non-breeding areas (Australia)

THE UNIVERSITY OF QUEENSLAND
AUSTRALIA

Figure 3. Migratory bird route over Japan. Source: R. Fuller School of Biological Sciences, University of Queensland, St Lucia, Qld 4072, Australia

Another source of funding for government is to reduce Japan's importation of energy. Japan currently imports 78% of its energy. Alternative energy contributes less than 1.5% of Japan's current electricity supply[xxxii]. Having 35% of Japan's energy needs being met by renewable sources could be achieved before 2030 if government approvals are speeded up. Much of the necessary environmental information such as bird migration routes[xxxiii], is available and should be used as a guide to prevent windmills from being located in certain areas[xxxiv] (see Figure 3).

Japan can be a pioneer in creating sound technology to prevent birds from flying too close to windmills. One study suggested an acoustic cue could be added to the blades that birds would hear. Some sounds (2 – 4 kHz) would not annoy humans but might help birds avoid the blades[xxxv]. Hodos tested various visual deterrents[xxxvi] but his report indicated a definite opportunity for science, including Japanese science to produce a fail-safe deterrent. Japanese kite technology could be used to develop airborne wind turbines. Scientists from Delft University of Technology in the Netherlands used a 10-sq metre high-altitude kite tethered to a generator, to produce 10 kilowatts of power, or enough for ten homes[xxxvii]. The project, called Laddermill, was headed by Professor Wubbo Ockels.

Hydropower is the leading source of renewable energy In Japan, producing about 22 GW at approximately 1,859 sites[xxxviii] with 26 sites under construction and 2,714 untapped. There are small hydropower projects in Yamanashi prefecture and large projects in Kanagawa prefecture. Hydropower is suited to Japan and threr are many utility companies, firms, and government agencies involved such as Hitachi Limited (NYSE:HIT) (Tokyo), Mitsubishi Electric Corporation (TYO:6503) (Tokyo), and Mitsubishi Heavy Industries Limited (MHI) (TYO:7011) (Tokyo). Japan's feed-in tariff system obliges Japan's 10 regional power utilities to buy electricity generated by solar and wind projects, paying about ¥40 (50 cents) per kilowatt-hour and ¥23 per kilowatt-hour, respectively. Solar tariff payments are set for 20 years, wind tariff payments for 15 (Iwata, 2012).

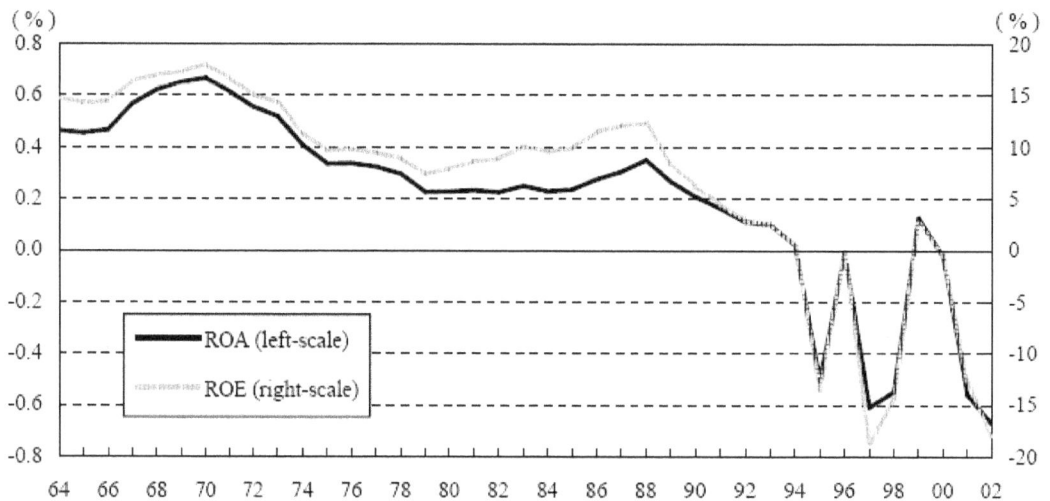

Sources: Japanese Bankers Association, Financial Statements of All Banks.
Notes: 1. Figures are for domestically licensed banks (summation of city banks, regional banks, regional banks II, trust banks, and long-term credit banks).
2. The definitions of ROA and ROE are as follows:
ROA = (Profit for the Term)/(Total Assets − Acceptance and Guarantees)
ROE = (Profit for the Term)/(Total Stockholders' Equity)

Figure 4. Profitability of Japanese Banks

Professor Toshihiro Ihori of the University of Tokyo told the New York Times that the US was correct in spending more money on energy and information-technology infrastructure and implied that Japan should do the same.

Nakanunara, nakumadematou, hototogisu (If the cuckoo does not sing, wait for it).

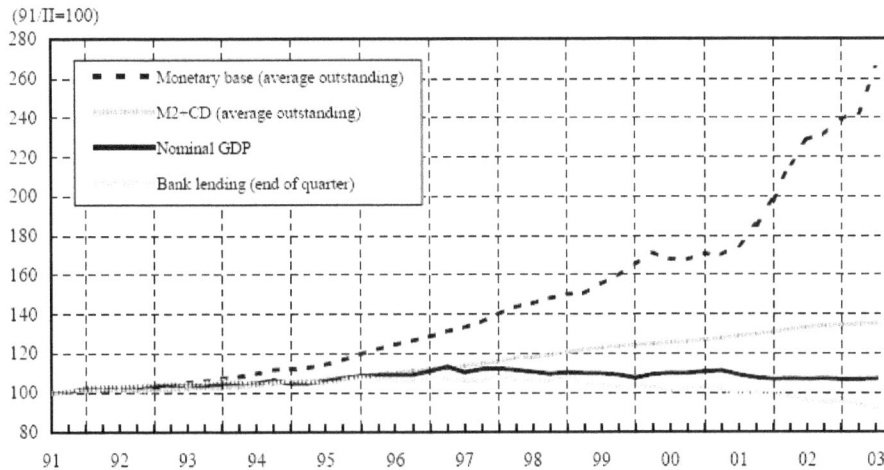

Figure 5. Lending of Japanese Banks

Japan in the future can have a smaller population, with more land area, more space for wild animals and for livestock rearing. A smaller global population means more fish in the sea and a reduced need for nuclear energy. Japan's population density is one of the highest in the world and this can produce negative health effects, for example many Japanese people wear face masks to avoid spreading or catching diseases. This is not common outside of Asia.

A future Japan can emulate the self-sufficiency of the Edo period. Japan's population at that time was 30 million. A reduction in population should alleviate environmental concerns and reduce the possible negative effects of climate change on Japan. These effects are said to include an increase in temperature of 1 to 3 degrees Celsius; a change in the growing season, reduced fresh water in some places and reduced rice yields[xxxix]. Traditional folk tales of Japan show that mothers of many children can be evil while those with one child can raise a heroic child who will be economically successful enough to care for his parents in old age. There are several of these stories; perhaps Japan can take a greater lead in research on extending fertility. Fertility for men and women declines slowly after age 30 and more rapidly after age 40. There are several studies on Asian herbs used for fertility such as senrigoma (*Rehmannia glutinosa*), shakuyaku (*Paenoia lactiflora*), gaiyou (*Artemisia argyi*), dong quai (*Angelica sinensis*), kanzō (*Glycyrrhiza uralensis*), and kouhon (*Ligusticum sinense*).

Japan can also take the lead in the developing field of research on healthy aging which could include alleviating the pains of old age through acupuncture, proper diet and exercise. Research could also include investigating the medicinal properties of the peach. It has traditionally been a symbol of long life and happy marriages. Perhaps it influences fertility since it served as the symbolic womb of Momotaro in the story *'Momotaro, or the story of the son of a peach*[xl].

The Edo period and Japan's fables provide a model for a sustainable Japan

i Hearne, Lafcadio. 1898 [1924]. Japanese fairy tales. Boni and Liveright.

ii Source: U.S. Census Bureau, International Data Base.

iii Ishikawa, E. The Edo Period had a Recycling Society (O-edo recycle jijo, published in 1994 by Kodansha Publishing Company).

iv Agri-food consumer profile Japan, May 2011. Available online at http://www.ats-sea.agr.gc.ca/asi/4150-eng.htm. Accessed August 26, 2012

v Associated Press. 2012. Japan reports $6.5 billion trade deficit in July, as exports sink, fuel imports surge. The Washington Post, August 22, 2012. Accessed August 26, 2012. http://www.washingtonpost.com/business/japan-reports-65-billion-trade-deficit-in-july-as-exports-sink-fuel-imports-surge/2012/08/21/884bc334-ebf1-11e1-866f-60a00f604425_story.html

vi Law, Jane Marie. 1997. *Puppets of Nostalgia: The Life, Death, and Rebirth of the Japanese Awaji Ningyo Tradition* Princeton University Press.

vii Horioka C.Y., Suzuki W., Hatta T. 2007. Aging, savings, and public pensions in Japan. Asian Economic Policy Review 2 (2), 303 – 319. Accessed August 26, 2012..Available at *www.nber.org/papers/w13273*

viii Raines, David. 2007. The Evolution of Japanese Employer-Sponsored Retirement Plans. Social Security Bulletin, Vol. 67, No. 3, pp. 89-104, 2007. Accessed August 26, 2012.
Available at SSRN: http://ssrn.com/abstract=1154007http://www.ssa.gov/policy/docs/ssb/v67n3/v67n3p89.html

ix Sharp, Andy. 2012. Japan's population declines by record in challenge for growth. Bloomberg April 17, 2012. Accessed August 26, 2012.

x Usuki, Masaharu. Recent Changes to Retirement Benefits in Japan and Relevant Public Policy Issues. Working Paper, NLI Research Institute, Tokyo, February 2003. Accessed August 26, 2012. Available at *hermes-ir.lib.hit-u.ac.jp/rs/bitstream/10086/14440/1/pie_dp135.pdf*

xi Iwata, M., and Nishizawa A. 2008. Poverty and Social Welfare in Japan. Trans Pacific Press, Melbourne, 2008.

xii Connelly, Matthew. 2008. Fatal Misconception: The Struggle to Control World Population. *Harvard University Press (Belknap).*

xiii Gardiner, A.B. 2010. Global population control: Not dead yet. New Oxford Book Reviews April 2012. Accessed on August 28, 2012. Available at. http://www.newoxfordreview.org/reviews.jsp?did=0410-gardiner.

xiv Kim, Anna M. 2009. Book review. *The Political Economy of Japan's Low Fertility* Frances McCall Rosenbluth (edited) Stanford University Press, 2007 xii+222 ISBN: 978-0-8047-5486-6 (hardback). Population Review 48 (1): 138-142.

xv Hirouki, Ida. 2004. Japanese Women in Their 30's:Changes and Traditional Values. "DAWN" Newsletter of the DAWN CENTER. December 2004. Accessed August 26, 2012. http://www.dawncenter.or.jp/english/publication/edawn/0412/01.html

xvi Ozaki, Y. 1908. *Japanese Fairy Tales*. (Lit2Go ed.). Retrieved August 26, 2012, from http://etc.usf.edu/lit2go/72/japanese-fairy-tales/

xvii http://durendal.org/jft/jft248.html

xviii Shelley, W.B. 1964. *Birch pollen and aspirin psoriasis: A study in salicylate* hypersensitivity JAMA Sep 28;189:985-8.

xix Roark, Anne. 2009. Day care for all ages. New York Times. Accessed August 26, 2012. http://newoldage.blogs.nytimes.com/2009/06/17/day-care-for-all-ages/

xx Nintendo 3DS – Health & Safety precautions. Accessed August 26, 2012.http://www.nintendo.com/consumer/systems/3ds/en_na/health_safety.jsp

[xxi] The point that salarymen are recruited through alumni networks but not necessarily matched to the most suitable job is made by Yoshimura Noboru and Anderson, Philip. 1997. Inside the Kaisha: Demystifying Japanese Business Behavior. Harvard Business School Press.

[xxii] Peng, Ito. 2002. Gender and welfare state restructuring in Japan. In C. Aspalter (ed.). Discovering the welfare state in East Asia. Westport, CT. Praeger Publishers, pp. 39=62..

[xxiii] Hayashi, Yuka. 2012. Welfare payments spur Japan debate. The Wall Street Journal June 7, 2012. Accessed August 26, 2012. Available online at http://online.wsj.com/article/SB10001424052702303296604577449731690922766.html..

[xxiv] Hay, J. 2009. Infrastructure and public works in Japan. Accessed August 28, 2012. Available online at http://factsanddetails.com/japan.php?itemid=842&catid=23&subcatid=152

[xxv] Fackler, M. 2009. Japan's big-works stimulus is lesson. The New York Times February 5, 2009. Accessed August 28, 2012. Available online at: http://www.nytimes.com/2009/02/06/world/asia/06japan.html?pagewanted=all.

[xxvi] Inagaki, K.,and Fukase, A. 2012. Cash-rich Japanese firms go on global buying spree. The Wall Street Journal May 29, 2012. Accessed August 26, 2012. Available online at http://online.wsj.com/article/SB10001424052702303505504577403743150818820.html.

[xxvii] Can America Compete? Strategies for economic revival. Feature. September – October 2012. Accessed August 26, 2012. Available online at http://harvardmagazine.com/2012/09/can-america-compete

[xxviii] Onaran, Y. 2012. *Zombie Banks: How Broken Banks And Debtor Nations Are Crippling the Global Economy* Bloomberg Press

[xxix] Bongaarts, J. 2004. Population aging and the rising cost of public pensions. *Policy Research Division Working Paper* (no. 185). Accessed August 26, 2012. Available at http://www.popcouncil.org/pdfs/wp/185.pdf

[xxx] Fukase, A. 2012. Profits rise at Japan's biggest banks. The Wall Street Journal May 15, 2012. Accessed on August 27, 2012. Online at http://online.wsj.com/article/SB10001424052702304371504577405871485099252.html

[xxxi] Source for Figures 4 and 5. Accessed August 26, 2012 .Available at: http://www.mybudget360.com/following-the-failed-japanese-economic-playbook-10-charts-comparing-the-japanese-lost-decade-to-the-united-states/

[xxxii] Yamamoto, E. 2007. Status of hydropower in Japan. Accessed August 26, 2012. *www.nef.or.jp/topics/pdf/2007_workshop_canada_presen.pdf*

[xxxiii] Fuller, R. 2011. Meeting with the Ambassador Designate to Japan. School of Biological Sciences, University of Queensland, St Lucia, Qld 4072, Australia. Accessed August 28, 2012.

[xxxiv] Iwata, M. 2012. Japanese solar power outlook looks bright but wind may not fly. Wall Street Journal August6 21, 2012. Accessed August 28, 2012. Available online at http://online.wsj.com/article/SB10000872396390443855804577602612914224228.html.

[xxxv] Dooling, R. 2002. Avian hearing and the avoidance of wind turbines. National Renewable Energy Laboratory, NREL/TP-500-30844. Accessed on August 28, 2012. Available at *www.nrel.gov/**wind**/pdfs/30844.pdf*

[xxxvi] Hodos, W. 2003. Minimization of motion smear: reducing avian collisions with wind turbines. Period of performance: 12 July 1999 to 31 August 2002. United States Department of Energy, National Renewable Energy Laboratory Technical Report NREL/SR-500–33249, Golden, Colorado, USA.

[xxxvii] Jha, Alok. 2008. Giant kites to tap power of the high wind. The Guardian online. August 3, 2008. Accessed August 28, 2012. Available online at: http://www.guardian.co.uk/environment/2008/aug/03/renewableenergy.energy

[xxxviii] Hydropower Could Become More Prevalent in Japan Following Nuclear Crisis, an Industrial Info News Alert. Accessed on August 28, 2012. Full report at http://www.industrialinfo.com/showNews.jsp?newsitemID=178310. News Alert available at.

http://www.marketwire.com/press-release/hydropower-could-become-more-prevalent-japan-following-nuclear-crisis-industrial-info-1508440.htm

[xxxix] WWF Global. Climate change impacts in Japan. Highlights of the IPCC 4th Assessment Report 2007. Accessed August 28, 2012. Available online at:

http://wwf.panda.org/about_our_earth/aboutcc/problems/rising_temperatures/hotspot_map/japan.cfm

[xl] http://durendal.org/jft/jft282.html.

Japanese: 『凱風快晴』 - Gaifū kaisei

South Wind, Clear Sky

The Project Gutenberg EBook of Japanese Fairy Tales, by Yei Theodora Ozaki

Title: Japanese Fairy Tales

Author: Yei Theodora Ozaki

Posting Date: June 4, 2009 [EBook #4018] Release Date: May, 2003
First Posted: October 11, 2001

The Edo period and Japan's fables provide a model for a sustainable Japan

THE TONGUE-CUT SPARROW

Shita-kiri Suzume (舌切り雀 *shita-kiri suzume*[?]), translated literally into "**Tongue-Cut Sparrow**", is a traditional Japanese fable.

Once upon a time there lived a poor old woodcutter with his wife, who earned their living by cutting wood and fishing. The old man was honest and kind but his wife was arrogant and greedy. One morning, the old man went into the mountains to cut timber and saw an injured sparrow crying out for help. Feeling sorry for the bird, the man takes it back to his home and feeds it some rice to try to help it recover. His wife, being very greedy and rude, is annoyed that he would waste precious food on such a small little thing as a sparrow. The old man, however, continued caring for the bird.

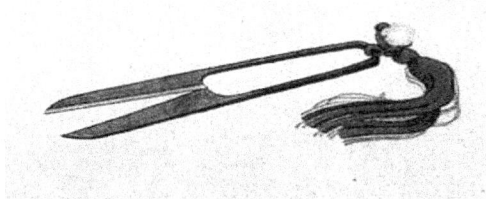

Katsushika Hokusai (葛飾北斎) (1760–1849) *Pair of scissors and sparrow*

The man had to return to the mountains one day and left the bird in the care of the old woman, who had no intention of feeding it. After her husband left, she went out fishing. While she was gone, the sparrow got into some starch that was left out and eventually ate all of it. The old woman was so angry upon her return that she cut out the bird's tongue and sent it flying back into the mountains from where it came.

The old man went searching for the bird and, with the help of other sparrows, found his way into a bamboo grove in which the sparrow's inn was located. A multitude of sparrows greeted him and led him to his friend, the little sparrow he saved. The others brought him food and sang and danced for him. Upon his departure, they presented him with a choice of a large basket or a small basket as a present. Being an older man, he chose the small basket as he thought it would be the least heavy. When he arrived home, he opened the basket and discovered a large amount of treasure inside. The wife, learning of the existence of a larger basket, ran to the sparrow's inn in the hope of getting more treasure for herself. She chose the larger basket but was warned not to open it before getting home. Such was her greed that the wife could not resist opening the basket before she returned to the house. To her surprise, the box was full of deadly snakes and other monsters. They startled her so much that she tumbled all the way down the mountain, presumably to her death.

Japanese: 『甲州伊沢暁』 - Kōshū Isawa no Akatsuki
Dawn at Isawa in Kai Province

The Edo period and Japan's fables provide a model for a sustainable Japan

Kitagawa Utamaro, Yama-uba and Kintaro

Hiroshige (1797–1858), Japanese woodblock print of Mt. Fuji and Mt. Ashigara viewed from Numazu in clear weather after a snowfall.

A young Kintarō battling a giant carp by Yoshitoshi.

THE ADVENTURES OF KINTARO, THE GOLDEN BOY.

http://www.gutenberg.org/files/4018/4018-h/4018-h.htm#kintaro

Long, long ago there lived in Kyoto a brave soldier named Kintoki. Now he fell in love with a beautiful lady and married her. Not long after this, through the malice of some of his friends, he fell into disgrace at Court and was dismissed. This misfortune so preyed upon his mind that he did not long survive his dismissal—he died, leaving behind him his beautiful young wife to face the world alone. Fearing her husband's enemies, she fled to the Ashigara Mountains as soon as her husband was dead, and there in the lonely forests where no one ever came except woodcutters, a little boy was born to her. She called him Kintaro or the Golden Boy. Now the remarkable thing about this child was his great strength, and as he grew older he grew stronger and stronger, so that by the time he was eight years of age he was able to cut down trees as quickly as the woodcutters. Then his mother gave him a large ax, and he used to go out in the forest and help the woodcutters, who called him "Wonder-child," and his mother the "Old Nurse of the Mountains," for they did not know her high rank. Another favorite pastime of Kintaro's was to smash up rocks and stones. You can imagine how strong he was!

Quite unlike other boys, Kintaro, grew up all alone in the mountain wilds, and as he had no companions he made friends with all the animals and learned to understand them and to speak their strange talk. By degrees they all grew quite tame and looked upon Kintaro as their master, and he used them as his servants and messengers. But his special retainers were the bear, the deer, the monkey and the hare.

The bear often brought her cubs for Kintaro to romp with, and when she came to take them home Kintaro would get on her back and have a ride to her cave. He was very fond of the deer too, and would often put his arms round the creature's neck to show that its long horns did not frighten him. Great was the fun they all had together.

One day, as usual, Kintaro went up into the mountains, followed by the bear, the deer, the monkey, and the hare. After walking for some time up hill and down dale and over rough roads, they suddenly came out upon a wide and grassy plain covered with pretty wild flowers.

Here, indeed, was a nice place where they could all have a good romp together. The deer rubbed his horns against a tree for pleasure, the monkey scratched his back, the hare smoothed his long ears, and the bear gave a grunt of satisfaction.

Kintaro said, "Here is a place for a good game. What do you all say to a wrestling match?"

The bear being the biggest and the oldest, answered for the others:

"That will be great fun," said she. "I am the strongest animal, so I will make the platform for the wrestlers;" and she set to work with a will to dig up the earth and to pat it into shape.

"All right," said Kintaro, "I will look on while you all wrestle with each other. I shall give a prize to the one who wins in each round."

"What fun! we shall all try to get the prize," said the bear.

The deer, the monkey and the hare set to work to help the bear raise the platform on which they were all to wrestle. When this was finished, Kintaro cried out:

"Now begin! the monkey and the hare shall open the sports and the deer shall be umpire. Now, Mr. Deer, you are to be umpire!"

"He, he!" answered the deer. "I will be umpire. Now, Mr. Monkey and Mr. Hare, if you are both ready, please walk out and take your places on the platform."

Then the monkey and the hare both hopped out, quickly and nimbly, to the wrestling platform. The deer, as umpire, stood between the two and called out:

"Red-back! Red-back!" (this to the monkey, who has a red back in Japan). "Are you ready?"

Then he turned to the hare:

"Long-ears! Long-ears! are you ready?"

Both the little wrestlers faced each other while the deer raised a leaf on high as signal. When he dropped the leaf the monkey and the hare rushed upon each other, crying "Yoisho, yoisho!"

While the monkey and the hare wrestled, the deer called out encouragingly or shouted warnings to each of them as the hare or the monkey pushed each other near the edge of the platform and were in danger of falling over.

"Red-back! Red-back! stand your ground!" called out the deer.

"Long-ears! Long-ears! be strong, be strong—don't let the monkey beat you!" grunted the bear.

So the monkey and the hare, encouraged by their friends, tried their very hardest to beat each other. The hare at last gained on the monkey. The monkey seemed to trip up, and the hare giving him a good push sent him flying off the platform with a bound.

The poor monkey sat up rubbing his back, and his face was very long as he screamed angrily. "Oh, oh! how my back hurts—my back hurts me!"

Seeing the monkey in this plight on the ground, the deer holding his leaf on high said:

"This round is finished—the hare has won."

Kintaro then opened his luncheon box and taking out a rice-dumpling, gave it to the hare saying:

"Here is your prize, and you have earned, it well!"

Now the monkey got up looking very cross, and as they say in Japan "his stomach stood up," for he felt that he had not been fairly beaten. So he said to Kintaro and the others who were standing by:

"I have not been fairly beaten. My foot slipped and I tumbled. Please give me another chance and let the hare wrestle with me for another round."

Then Kintaro consenting, the hare and the monkey began to wrestle again. Now, as every one knows, the monkey is a cunning animal by nature, and he made up his mind to get the best of the hare this time if it were possible. To do this, he thought that the best and surest way would be to get hold of the hare's long ear. This he soon managed to do. The hare was quite thrown off his guard by the pain of having his long ear pulled so hard, and the monkey seizing his opportunity at last, caught hold of one of the hare's legs and sent him sprawling in the middle of the dais. The monkey was now the victor and received, a rice-dumpling from Kintaro, which pleased him so much that he quite forgot his sore back.

The deer now came up and asked the hare if he felt ready for another round, and if so whether he would try a round with him, and the hare consenting, they both stood up to wrestle. The bear came forward as umpire.

The deer with long horns and the hare with long ears, it must have been an amusing sight to those who watched this queer match. Suddenly the deer went down on one of his knees, and the bear with the leaf on high declared him beaten. In this way, sometimes the one, sometimes the other, conquering, the little party amused themselves till they were tired.

At last Kintaro got up and said:

"This is enough for to-day. What a nice place we have found for wrestling; let us come again to-morrow. Now, we will all go home. Come along!" So saying, Kintaro led the way while the animals followed.

After walking some little distance they came out on the banks of a river flowing through a valley. Kintaro and his four furry friends stood and looked about for some means of crossing. Bridge there was none. The river rushed "don, don" on its way. All the animals looked serious, wondering how they could cross the stream and get home that evening.

Kintaro, however, said:

"Wait a moment. I will make a good bridge for you all in a few minutes."

The bear, the deer, the monkey and the hare looked at him to see what he would do now.

Kintaro went from one tree to another that grew along the river bank. At last he stopped in front of a very large tree that was growing at the water's edge. He took hold of the trunk and pulled it with all his might, once, twice, thrice! At the third pull, so great was Kintaro's strength that the roots gave way, and "meri, meri" (crash, crash), over fell the tree, forming an excellent bridge across the stream.

"There," said Kintaro, "what do you think of my bridge? It is quite safe, so follow me," and he stepped across first. The four animals followed. Never had they seen any one so strong before, and they all exclaimed:

"How strong he is! how strong he is!"

While all this was going on by the river a woodcutter, who happened to be standing on a rock overlooking the stream, had seen all that passed beneath him. He watched with great surprise Kintaro and his animal companions. He rubbed his eyes to be sure that he was not dreaming when he saw this boy pull over a tree by the roots and throw it across the stream to form a bridge.

The woodcutter, for such he seemed to be by his dress, marveled at all he saw, and said to himself:

"This is no ordinary child. Whose son can he be? I will find out before this day is done."

He hastened after the strange party and crossed the bridge behind them. Kintaro knew nothing of all this, and little guessed that he was being followed. On reaching the other side of the river he and the animals separated, they to their lairs in the woods and he to his mother, who was waiting for him.

As soon as he entered the cottage, which stood like a matchbox in the heart of the pine-woods, he went to greet his mother, saying:

"Okkasan (mother), here I am!"

"O, Kimbo!" said his mother with a bright smile, glad to see her boy home safe after the long day. "How late you are to-day. I feared that something had happened to you. Where have you been all the time?"

"I took my four friends, the bear, the deer, the monkey, and the hare, up into the hills, and there I made them try a wrestling match, to see which was the strongest. We all enjoyed the sport, and are going to the same place to-morrow to have another match."

"Now tell me who is the strongest of all?" asked his mother, pretending not to know.

"Oh, mother," said Kintaro, "don't you know that I am the strongest? There was no need for me to wrestle with any of them."

"But next to you then, who is the strongest?"

"The bear comes next to me in strength," answered Kintaro.

"And after the bear?" asked his mother again.

"Next to the bear it is not easy to say which is the strongest, for the deer, the monkey, and the hare all seem to be as strong as each other," said Kintaro.

Suddenly Kintaro and his mother were startled by a voice from outside.

"Listen to me, little boy! Next time you go, take this old man with you to the wrestling match. He would like to join the sport too!"

It was the old woodcutter who had followed Kintaro from the river. He slipped off his clogs and entered the cottage. Yama-uba and her son were both taken by surprise. They looked at the intruder wonderingly and saw that he was some one they had never seen before.

"Who are you?" they both exclaimed.

Then the woodcutter laughed and said:

"It does not matter who I am yet, but let us see who has the strongest arm—this boy or myself?"

Then Kintaro, who had lived all his life in the forest, answered the old man without any ceremony, saying:

"We will have a try if you wish it, but you must not be angry whoever is beaten."

Then Kintaro and the woodcutter both put out their right arms and grasped each other's hands. For a long time Kintaro and the old man wrestled together in this way, each trying to bend the other's arm, but the old man was very strong, and the strange pair were evenly matched. At last the old man desisted, declaring it a drawn game.

"You are, indeed, a very strong child. There are few men who can boast of the strength of my right arm!" said the woodcutter. "I saw you first on the hanks of the river a few hours ago, when you pulled up that large tree to make a bridge across the torrent. Hardly able to believe what I saw I followed you home. Your strength of arm, which I have just tried, proves what I saw this afternoon. When you are full-grown you will surely be the strongest man in all Japan. It is a pity that you are hidden away in these wild mountains."

Then he turned to Kintaro's mother:

"And you, mother, have you no thought of taking your child to the Capital, and of teaching him to carry a sword as befits a samurai (a Japanese knight)?"

"You are very kind to take so much interest in my son." replied the mother; "but he is as you see, wild and uneducated, and I fear it would be very difficult to do as you say. Because of his great strength as an infant I hid him away in this unknown part of the country, for he hurt every one that came near him. I have often wished that I could, one day, see my boy a knight wearing two swords, but as we have no influential friend to introduce us at the Capital, I fear my hope will never come true."

"You need not trouble yourself about that. To tell you the truth I am no woodcutter! I am one of the great generals of Japan. My name is Sadamitsu, and I am a vassal of the powerful Lord Minamoto-no-Raiko. He ordered me to go round the country and look for boys who give promise of remarkable strength, so that they may be trained as soldiers for his army. I thought that I could best do this by assuming the disguise of a woodcutter. By good fortune, I have thus unexpectedly come across your son. Now if you really wish him to be a SAMURAI (a knight), I will take him and present him to the Lord Raiko as a candidate for his service. What do you say to this?"

As the kind general gradually unfolded his plan the mother's heart was filled with a great joy. She saw that here was a wonderful chance of the one wish of her life being fulfilled—that of seeing Kintaro a SAMURAI before she died.

Bowing her head to the ground, she replied:

"I will then intrust my son to you if you really mean what you say."

Kintaro had all this time been sitting by his mother's side listening to what they said. When his mother finished speaking, he exclaimed:

"Oh, joy! joy! I am to go with the general and one day I shall be a SAMURAI!"

Thus Kintaro's fate was settled, and the general decided to start for the Capital at once, taking Kintaro with him. It need hardly be said that Yama-uba was sad at parting with her boy, for he was all that was left to her. But she hid her grief with a strong face, as they say in Japan. She knew that it was for her boy's good that he should leave her now, and she must not discourage him just as he was setting out. Kintaro promised never to forget her, and said that as soon as he was a knight wearing two swords he would build her a home and take care of her in her old age.

All the animals, those he had tamed to serve him, the bear, the deer, the monkey, and the hare, as soon as they found out that he was going away, came to ask if they might attend him as usual. When they learned that he was going away for good they followed him to the foot of the mountain to see him off.

"Kimbo," said his mother, "mind and be a good boy."

"Mr. Kintaro," said the faithful animals, "we wish you good health on your travels."

Then they all climbed a tree to see the last of him, and from that height they watched him and his shadow gradually grow smaller and smaller, till he was lost to sight.

The general Sadamitsu went on his way rejoicing at having so unexpectedly found such a prodigy as Kintaro.

Having arrived at their destination the general took Kintaro at once to his Lord, Minamoto-no-Raiko, and told him all about Kintaro and how he had found the child. Lord Raiko was delighted with the story, and having commanded Kintaro to be brought to him, made him one of his vassals at once.

Lord Raiko's army was famous for its band called "The Four Braves." These warriors were chosen by himself from amongst the bravest and strongest of his soldiers, and the small and well-picked band was distinguished throughout the whole of Japan for the dauntless courage of its men.

When Kintaro grew up to be a man his master made him the Chief of the Four Braves. He was by far the strongest of them all. Soon after this event, news was brought to the city that a cannibal monster had taken up his abode not far away and that people were stricken with fear. Lord Raiko ordered Kintaro to the rescue. He immediately started off, delighted at the prospect of trying his sword.

Surprising the monster in its den, he made short work of cutting off its great head, which he carried back in triumph to his master.

Kintaro now rose to be the greatest hero of his country, and great was the power and honor and wealth that came to him. He now kept his promise and built a comfortable home for his old mother, who lived happily with him in the Capital to the end of her days.

Is not this the story of a great hero?

The Edo period and Japan's fables provide a model for a sustainable Japan

17th century reproduction from a book showing The Tale of the Bamboo Cutter
Hiroshige (179701858). Old Bamboo Cutter and Princess Kaguya, The Moon Child

http://www.metmuseum.org/Collections/search-the-collections/60013157?rpp=60&pg=1&gallerynos=228&ft=*&pos=1

http://www.gutenberg.org/files/4018/4018-h/4018-h.htm#bamboo

THE BAMBOO-CUTTER AND THE MOON-CHILD.

Long, long ago, there lived an old bamboo wood-cutter. He was very poor and sad also, for no child had Heaven sent to cheer his old age, and in his heart there was no hope of rest from work till he died and was laid in the quiet grave. Every morning he went forth into the woods and hills wherever the bamboo reared its lithe green plumes against the sky. When he had made his choice, he would cut down these feathers of the forest, and splitting them lengthwise, or cutting them into joints, would carry the bamboo wood home and make it into various articles for the household, and he and his old wife gained a small livelihood by selling them.

One morning as usual he had gone out to his work, and having found a nice clump of bamboos, had set to work to cut some of them down. Suddenly the green grove of bamboos was flooded with a bright soft light, as if the full moon had risen over the spot. Looking round in astonishment, he saw that the brilliance was streaming from one bamboo. The old man, full of wonder, dropped his ax and went towards the light. On nearer approach he saw that this soft splendor came from a hollow in the green bamboo stem, and still more wonderful to behold, in the midst of the brilliance stood a tiny human being, only three inches in height, and exquisitely beautiful in appearance.

"You must be sent to be my child, for I find you here among the bamboos where lies my daily work," said the old man, and taking the little creature in his hand he took it home to his wife to bring up. The tiny girl was so exceedingly beautiful and so small, that the old woman put her into a basket to safeguard her from the least possibility of being hurt in any way. The old couple were now very happy, for it had been a lifelong regret that they had no children of their own, and with joy they now expended all the love of their old age on the little child who had come to them in so marvelous a manner. From this time on, the old man often found gold in the notches of the bamboos when he hewed them down and cut them up; not only gold, but precious stones also, so that by degrees he became rich. He built himself a fine house, and was no longer known as the poor bamboo woodcutter, but as a wealthy man.

Three months passed quickly away, and in that time the bamboo child had, wonderful to say, become a full-grown girl, so her foster-parents did up her hair and dressed her in beautiful kimonos. She was of such wondrous beauty that they placed her behind the screens like a princess, and allowed no one to see her, waiting upon her themselves. It seemed as if she were made of light, for the house was filled with a soft shining, so that even in the dark of night it was like daytime. Her presence seemed to have a benign influence on those there. Whenever the old man felt sad, he had only to look upon his foster-daughter and his sorrow vanished, and he became as happy as when he was a youth.

At last the day came for the naming of their new-found child, so the old couple called in a celebrated name-giver, and he gave her the name of Princess Moonlight, because her body gave forth so much soft bright light that she might have been a daughter of the Moon God.

For three days the festival was kept up with song and dance and music. All the friends and relations of the old couple were present, and great was their enjoyment of the festivities held to celebrate the naming of Princess Moonlight. Everyone who saw her declared that there never had been seen any one so lovely; all the beauties throughout the length and breadth of the land would grow pale beside her, so they said. The fame of the Princess's loveliness spread far and wide, and many were the suitors who desired to win her hand, or even so much as to see her.

Suitors from far and near posted themselves outside the house, and made little holes in the fence, in the hope of catching a glimpse of the Princess as she went from one room to the other along the veranda. They stayed there day and night, sacrificing even their sleep for a chance of seeing her, but all in vain. Then they approached the house, and tried to speak to the old man and his wife or some of the servants, but not even this was granted them.

Still, in spite of all this disappointment they stayed on day after day, and night after night, and counted it as nothing, so great was their desire to see the Princess.

At last, however, most of the men, seeing how hopeless their quest was, lost heart and hope both, and returned to their homes. All except five Knights, whose ardor and determination, instead of waning, seemed to wax greater with obstacles. These five men even went without their meals, and took snatches of whatever they could get brought to them, so that they might always stand outside the dwelling. They stood there in all weathers, in sunshine and in rain.

Sometimes they wrote letters to the Princess, but no answer was vouchsafed to them. Then when letters failed to draw any reply, they wrote poems to her telling her of the hopeless love which kept them from sleep, from food, from rest, and even from their homes. Still Princes Moonlight gave no sign of having received their verses. In this hopeless state the winter passed. The snow and frost and the cold winds gradually gave place to the gentle warmth of spring. Then the summer came, and the sun burned white and scorching in the heavens above and on the earth beneath, and still these faithful Knights kept watch and waited. At the end of these long months they called out to the old bamboo-cutter and entreated him to have some mercy upon them and to show them the Princess, but he answered only that as he was not her real father he could not insist on her obeying him against her wishes.

The five Knights on receiving this stern answer returned to their several homes, and pondered over the best means of touching the proud Princess's heart, even so much as to grant them a hearing. They took their rosaries in hand and knelt before their household shrines, and burned precious incense, praying to Buddha to give them their heart's desire. Thus several days passed, but even so they could not rest in their homes.

So again they set out for the bamboo-cutter's house. This time the old man came out to see them, and they asked him to let them know if it was the Princess's resolution never to see any man whatsoever, and they implored him to speak for them and to tell her the greatness of their love, and how long they had waited through the cold of winter and the heat of summer, sleepless and roofless through all weathers, without food and without rest, in the ardent hope of winning her, and they were willing to consider this long vigil as pleasure if she would but give them one chance of pleading their cause with her.

The old man lent a willing ear to their tale of love, for in his inmost heart he felt sorry for these faithful suitors and would have liked to see his lovely foster-daughter married to one of them. So he went in to Princess Moonlight and said reverently:

"Although you have always seemed to me to be a heavenly being, yet I have had the trouble of bringing you up as my own child and you have been glad of the protection of my roof. Will you refuse to do as I wish?"

Then Princess Moonlight replied that there was nothing she would not do for him, that she honored and loved him as her own father, and that as for herself she could not remember the time before she came to earth. The old man listened with great joy as she spoke these dutiful words. Then he told her how anxious he was to see her safely and happily married before he died.

"I am an old man, over seventy years of age, and my end may come any time now. It is necessary and right that you should see these five suitors and choose one of them."

"Oh, why," said the Princess in distress, "must I do this? I have no wish to marry now."

"I found you," answered the old man, "many years ago, when you were a little creature three inches high, in the midst of a great white light. The light streamed from the bamboo in which you were hid and led me to you. So I have always thought that you were more than mortal woman. While I am alive it is right for you to remain as you are if you wish to do so, but some day I shall cease to be and who will take care of you then? Therefore I pray you to meet these five brave men one at a time and make up your mind to marry one of them!"

Then the Princess answered that she felt sure that she was not as beautiful as perhaps report made her out to be, and that even if she consented to marry any one of them, not really knowing her before, his heart might change afterwards. So as she did not feel sure of them, even though her father told her they were worthy Knights, she did not feel it wise to see them.

"All you say is very reasonable," said the old man, "but what kind of men will you consent to see? I do not call these five men who have waited on you for months, light-hearted. They have stood outside this house through the winter and the summer, often denying themselves food and sleep so that they may win you. What more can you demand?"

Then Princess Moonlight said she must make further trial of their love before she would grant their request to interview her. The five warriors were to prove their love by each bringing her from distant countries something that she desired to possess.

That same evening the suitors arrived and began to play their flutes in turn, and to sing their self-composed songs telling of their great and tireless love. The bamboo-cutter went out to them and offered them his sympathy for all they had endured and all the patience they had shown in their desire to win his foster-daughter. Then he gave them her message, that she would consent to marry whosoever was successful in bringing her what she wanted. This was to test them.

The five all accepted the trial, and thought it an excellent plan, for it would prevent jealousy between them.

Princess Moonlight then sent word to the First Knight that she requested him to bring her the stone bowl which had belonged to Buddha in India.

The Second Knight was asked to go to the Mountain of Horai, said to be situated in the Eastern Sea, and to bring her a branch of the wonderful tree that grew on its summit. The roots of this tree were of silver, the trunk of gold, and the branches bore as fruit white jewels.

The Third Knight was told to go to China and search for the fire-rat and to bring her its skin.

The Fourth Knight was told to search for the dragon that carried on its head the stone radiating five colors and to bring the stone to her.

The Fifth Knight was to find the swallow which carried a shell in its stomach and to bring the shell to her.

The old man thought these very hard tasks and hesitated to carry the messages, but the Princess would make no other conditions. So her commands were issued word for word to the five men who, when they heard what was required of them, were all disheartened and disgusted at what seemed to them the impossibility of the tasks given them and returned to their own homes in despair. But after a time, when they thought of the Princess, the love in their hearts revived for her, and they resolved to make an attempt to get what she desired of them.

The First Knight sent word to the Princess that he was starting out that day on the quest of Buddha's bowl, and he hoped soon to bring it to her. But he had not the courage to go all the way to India, for in those days traveling was very difficult and full of danger, so he went to one of the temples in Kyoto and took a stone bowl from the altar there, paying the priest a large sum of money for it. He then wrapped it in a cloth of gold and, waiting quietly for three years, returned and carried it to the old man. Princess Moonlight wondered that the Knight should have returned so soon. She took the bowl from its gold wrapping, expecting it to make the room full of light, but it did not shine at all, so she knew that it was a sham thing and not the true bowl of Buddha. She returned it at once and refused to see him. The Knight threw the bowl away and returned to his home in despair. He gave up now all hopes of ever winning the Princess.

The Second Knight told his parents that he needed change of air for his health, for he was ashamed to tell them that love for the Princess Moonlight was the real cause of his leaving them. He then left his home, at the same time sending word to the Princess that he was setting out for Mount Horai in the hope of getting her a branch of the gold and silver tree which she so much wished to have. He only allowed his servants to accompany him half-way, and then sent them back. He reached the seashore and embarked on a small ship, and after sailing away for three days he landed and employed several carpenters to build him a house contrived in such a way that no one could get access to it. He then shut himself up with six skilled jewelers, and endeavored to make such a gold and silver branch as he thought would satisfy the Princess as having come from the wonderful tree growing on Mount Horai. Every one whom he had asked declared that Mount Horai belonged to the land of fable and not to fact.

When the branch was finished, he took his journey home and tried to make himself look as if he were wearied and worn out with travel. He put the jeweled branch into a lacquer box and carried it to the bamboo-cutter, begging him to present it to the Princess.

The old man was quite deceived by the travel-stained appearance of the Knight, and thought that he had only just returned from his long journey with the branch. So he tried to persuade the Princess to consent to see the man. But she remained silent and looked very sad. The old man began to take out the branch and praised it as a wonderful treasure to be found nowhere in the whole land. Then he spoke of the Knight, how handsome and how brave he was to have undertaken a journey to so remote a place as the Mount of Horai. Princess Moonlight took the branch in her hand and looked at it carefully. She then told her foster-parent that she knew it was impossible for the man to have obtained a branch from the gold and silver tree growing on Mount Horai so quickly or so easily, and she was sorry to say she believed it artificial.

The old man then went out to the expectant Knight, who had now approached the house, and asked where he had found the branch. Then the man did not scruple to make up a long story.

"Two years ago I took a ship and started in search of Mount Horai. After going before the wind for some time I reached the far Eastern Sea. Then a great storm arose and I was tossed about for many days, losing all count of the points of the compass, and finally we were blown ashore on an unknown island. Here I found the place inhabited by demons who at one time threatened to kill and eat me. However, I managed to make friends with these horrible creatures, and they helped me and my sailors to repair the boat, and I set sail again. Our food gave out, and we suffered much from sickness on board. At last, on the five-hundredth day from the day of starting, I saw far off on the horizon what looked like the peak of a mountain. On nearer approach, this proved to be an island, in the center of which rose a high mountain. I landed, and after wandering about for two or three days, I saw a shining being coming towards me on the beach, holding in his hands a golden bowl. I went up to him and asked him if I had, by good chance, found the island of Mount Horai, and he answered:"

"'Yes, this is Mount Horai!'"

"With much difficulty I climbed to the summit, here stood the golden tree growing with silver roots in the ground. The wonders of that strange land are many, and if I began to tell you about them I could never stop. In spite of my wish to stay there long, on breaking off the branch I hurried back. With utmost speed it has taken me four hundred days to get back, and, as you see, my clothes are still damp from exposure on the long sea voyage. I have not even waited to change my raiment, so anxious was I to bring the branch to the Princess quickly."

Just at this moment the six jewelers, who had been employed on the making of the branch, but not yet paid by the Knight, arrived at the house and sent in a petition to the Princess to be paid for their labor. They said that they had worked for over a thousand days making the branch of gold, with its silver twigs and its jeweled fruit, that was now presented to her by the Knight, but as yet they had received nothing in payment. So this Knight's deception was thus found out, and the Princess, glad of an escape from one more importunate suitor, was only too pleased to send back the branch. She called in the workmen and had them paid liberally, and they went away happy. But on the way home they were overtaken by the disappointed man, who beat them till they were nearly dead, for letting out the secret, and they barely escaped with their lives. The Knight then returned home, raging in his heart; and in despair of ever winning the Princess gave up society and retired to a solitary life among the mountains.

Now the Third Knight had a friend in China, so he wrote to him to get the skin of the fire-rat. The virtue of any part of this animal was that no fire could harm it. He promised his friend any amount of money he liked to ask if only he could get him the desired article. As soon as the news came that the ship on which his friend had sailed home had come into port, he rode seven days on horseback to meet him. He handed his friend a large sum of money, and received the fire-rat's skin. When he reached home he put it carefully in a box and sent it in to the Princess while he waited outside for her answer.

The bamboo-cutter took the box from the Knight and, as usual, carried it in to her and tried to coax her to see the Knight at once, but Princess Moonlight refused, saying that she must first put the skin to test by putting it into the fire. If it were the real thing it would not burn. So she took off the crape wrapper and opened the box, and then threw the skin into the fire. The skin crackled and burnt up at once, and the Princess knew that this man also had not fulfilled his word. So the Third Knight failed also. Now the Fourth Knight was no more enterprising than the rest. Instead of starting out on the quest of the dragon bearing on its head the five-color-radiating jewel, he called all his servants together and gave them the order to seek for it far and wide in Japan and in China, and he strictly forbade any of them to return till they had found it.

His numerous retainers and servants started out in different directions, with no intention, however, of obeying what they considered an impossible order. They simply took a holiday, went to pleasant country places together, and grumbled at their master's unreasonableness. The Knight meanwhile, thinking that his retainers could not fail to find the jewel, repaired to his house, and fitted it up beautifully for the reception of the Princess, he felt so sure of winning her.

One year passed away in weary waiting, and still his men did not return with the dragon-jewel. The Knight became desperate. He could wait no longer, so taking with him only two men he hired a ship and commanded the captain to go in search of the dragon; the captain and the sailors refused to undertake what they said was an absurd search, but the Knight compelled them at last to put out to sea.

When they had been but a few days out they encountered a great storm which lasted so long that, by the time its fury abated, the Knight had determined to give up the hunt of the dragon. They were at last blown on shore, for navigation was primitive in those days. Worn out with his travels and anxiety, the fourth suitor gave himself up to rest. He had caught a very heavy cold, and had to go to bed with a swollen face.

The governor of the place, hearing of his plight, sent messengers with a letter inviting him to his house. While he was there thinking over all his troubles, his love for the Princess turned to anger, and he blamed her for all the hardships he had undergone. He thought that it was quite probable she had wished to kill him so that she might be rid of him, and in order to carry out her wish had sent him upon his impossible quest. At this point all the servants he had sent out to find the jewel came to see him, and were surprised to find praise instead of displeasure awaiting them. Their master told them that he was heartily sick of adventure, and said that he never intended to go near the Princess's house again in the future.

Like all the rest, the Fifth Knight failed in his quest—he could not find the swallow's shell.

By this time the fame of Princess Moonlight's beauty had reached the ears of the Emperor, and he sent one of the Court ladies to see if she were really as lovely as report said; if so he would summon her to the Palace and make her one of the ladies-in-waiting. When the Court lady arrived, in spite of her father's entreaties, Princess Moonlight refused to see her. The Imperial messenger insisted, saying it was the Emperor's order. Then Princess Moonlight told the old man that if she was forced to go to the Palace in obedience to the Emperor's order, she would vanish from the earth.

When the Emperor was told of her persistence in refusing to obey his summons, and that if pressed to obey she would disappear altogether from sight, he determined to go and see her. So he planned to go on a hunting excursion in the neighborhood of the bamboo-cutter's house, and see the Princess himself. He sent word to the old man of his intention, and he received consent to the scheme. The next day the Emperor set out with his retinue, which he soon managed to outride. He found the bamboo-cutter's house and dismounted. He then entered the house and went straight to where the Princess was sitting with her attendant maidens.

Never had he seen any one so wonderfully beautiful, and he could not but look at her, for she was more lovely than any human being as she shone in her own soft radiance. When Princess Moonlight became aware that a stranger was looking at her she tried to escape from the room, but the Emperor caught her and begged her to listen to what he had to say. Her only answer was to hide her face in her sleeves.

The Emperor fell deeply in love with her, and begged her to come to the Court, where he would give her a position of honor and everything she could wish for. He was about to send for one of the Imperial palanquins to take her back with him at once, saying that her grace and beauty should adorn a Court, and not be hidden in a bamboo-cutter's cottage. But the Princess stopped him. She said that if she were forced to go to the Palace she would turn at once into a shadow, and even as she spoke she began to lose her form. Her figure faded from his sight while he looked.

The Emperor then promised to leave her free if only she would resume her former shape, which she did.

It was now time for him to return, for his retinue would be wondering what had happened to their Royal master when they missed him for so long. So he bade her good-by, and left the house with a sad heart. Princess Moonlight was for him the most beautiful woman in the world; all others were dark beside her, and he thought of her night and day. His Majesty now spent much of his time in writing poems, telling her of his love and devotion, and sent them to her, and though she refused to see him again she answered with many verses of her own composing, which told him gently and kindly that she could never marry any one on this earth. These little songs always gave him pleasure.

At this time her foster-parents noticed that night after night the Princess would sit on her balcony and gaze for hours at the moon, in a spirit of the deepest dejection, ending always in a burst of tears. One night the old man found her thus weeping as if her heart were broken, and he besought her to tell him the reason of her sorrow.

With many tears she told him that he had guessed rightly when he supposed her not to belong to this world—that she had in truth come from the moon, and that her time on earth would soon be over. On the fifteenth day of that very month of August her friends from the moon would come to fetch her, and she would have to return. Her parents were both there, but having spent a lifetime on the earth she had forgotten them, and also the moon-world to which she belonged. It made her weep, she said, to think of leaving her kind foster-parents, and the home where she had been happy for so long. When her attendants heard this they were very sad, and could not eat or drink for sadness at the thought that the Princess was so soon to leave them.

The Emperor, as soon as the news was carried to him, sent messengers to the house to find out if the report were true or not. The old bamboo-cutter went out to meet the Imperial messengers. The last few days of sorrow had told upon the old man; he had aged greatly, and looked much more than his seventy years. Weeping bitterly, he told them that the report was only too true, but he intended, however, to make prisoners of the envoys from the moon, and to do all he could to prevent the Princess from being carried back.

The men returned and told His Majesty all that had passed. On the fifteenth day of that month the Emperor sent a guard of two thousand warriors to watch the house. One thousand stationed themselves on the roof, another thousand kept watch round all the entrances of the house. All were well trained archers, with bows and arrows. The bamboo-cutter and his wife hid Princess Moonlight in an inner room.

The old man gave orders that no one was to sleep that night, all in the house were to keep a strict watch, and be ready to protect the Princess. With these precautions, and the help of the Emperor's men-at-arms, he hoped to withstand the moon-messengers, but the Princess told him that all these measures to keep her would be useless, and that when her people came for her nothing whatever could prevent them from carrying out their purpose. Even the Emperors men would be powerless. Then she added with tears that she was very, very sorry to leave him and his wife, whom she had learned to love as her parents, that if she could do as she liked she would stay with them in their old age, and try to make some return for all the love and kindness they had showered upon her during all her earthly life. The night wore on! The yellow harvest moon rose high in the heavens, flooding the world asleep with her golden light. Silence reigned over the pine and the bamboo forests, and on the roof where the thousand men-at-arms waited. Then the night grew gray towards the dawn and all hoped that the danger was over—that Princess Moonlight would not have to leave them after all. Then suddenly the watchers saw a cloud form round the moon—and while they looked this cloud began to roll earthwards. Nearer and nearer it came, and every one saw with dismay that its course lay towards the house.

In a short time the sky was entirely obscured, till at last the cloud lay over the dwelling only ten feet off the ground. In the midst of the cloud there stood a flying chariot, and in the chariot a band of luminous beings. One amongst them who looked like a king and appeared to be the chief stepped out of the chariot, and, poised in air, called to the old man to come out.

"The time has come," he said, "for Princess Moonlight to return to the moon from whence she came. She committed a grave fault, and as a punishment was sent to live down here for a time. We know what good care you have taken of the Princess, and we have rewarded you for this and have sent you wealth and prosperity. We put the gold in the bamboos for you to find."

"I have brought up this Princess for twenty years and never once has she done a wrong thing, therefore the lady you are seeking cannot be this one," said the old man. "I pray you to look elsewhere."

Then the messenger called aloud, saying:

"Princess Moonlight, come out from this lowly dwelling. Rest not here another moment."

At these words the screens of the Princess's room slid open of their own accord, revealing the Princess shining in her own radiance, bright and wonderful and full of beauty. The messenger led her forth and placed her in the chariot. She looked back, and saw with pity the deep sorrow of the old man. She spoke to him many comforting words, and told him that it was not her will to leave him and that he must always think of her when looking at the moon. The bamboo-cutter implored to be allowed to accompany her, but this was not allowed. The Princess took off her embroidered outer garment and gave it to him as a keepsake. One of the moon beings in the chariot held a wonderful coat of wings, another had a phial full of the Elixir of Life which was given the Princess to drink. She swallowed a little and was about to give the rest to the old man, but she was prevented from doing so.

The robe of wings was about to be put upon her shoulders, but she said:

"Wait a little. I must not forget my good friend the Emperor. I must write him once more to say good-by while still in this human form."

In spite of the impatience of the messengers and charioteers she kept them waiting while she wrote. She placed the phial of the Elixir of Life with the letter, and, giving them to the old man, she asked him to deliver them to the Emperor. Then the chariot began to roll heavenwards towards the moon, and as they all gazed with tearful eyes at the receding Princess, the dawn broke, and in the rosy light of day the moon-chariot and all in it were lost amongst the fleecy clouds that were now wafted across the sky on the wings of the morning wind. Princess Moonlight's letter was carried to the Palace. His Majesty was afraid to touch the Elixir of Life, so he sent it with the letter to the top of the most sacred mountain in the land. Mount Fuji, and there the Royal emissaries burnt it on the summit at sunrise. So to this day people say there is smoke to be seen rising from the top of Mount Fuji to the clouds.

Kaguya-hime goes back to the Moon Taketori Monogatari (竹取物語, The Tale of the Bamboo Cutter)

The Edo period and Japan's fables provide a model for a sustainable Japan

Violet Moore Higgins *The Silver Ship* 1916

1874 Wood Engraving Japan Japanese Woman Applying Makeup Kimono Mirror Brush

http://www.clas.ufl.edu/users/jshoaf/jdolls/jdollwestern/illustrations/books3ft.html

http://www.gutenberg.org/files/4018/4018-h/4018-h.htm#mirror

THE MIRROR OF MATSUYAMA A STORY OF OLD JAPAN.

Long years ago in old Japan there lived in the Province of Echigo, a very remote part of Japan even in these days, a man and his wife. When this story begins they had been married for some years and were blessed with one little daughter. She was the joy and pride of both their lives, and in her they stored an endless source of happiness for their old age.

What golden letter days in their memory were these that had marked her growing up from babyhood; the visit to the temple when she was just thirty days old, her proud mother carrying her, robed in ceremonial kimono, to be put under the patronage of the family's household god; then her first dolls festival, when her parents gave her a set of dolls' and their miniature belongings, to be added to as year succeeded year; and perhaps the most important occasion of all, on her third birthday, when her first OBI (broad brocade sash) of scarlet and gold was tied round her small waist, a sign that she had crossed the threshold of girlhood and left infancy behind. Now that she was seven years of age, and had learned to talk and to wait upon her parents in those several little ways so dear to the hearts of fond parents, their cup of happiness seemed full. There could not be found in the whole of the Island Empire a happier little family.

One day there was much excitement in the home, for the father had been suddenly summoned to the capital on business. In these days of railways and jinrickshas and other rapid modes of traveling, it is difficult to realize what such a journey as that from Matsuyama to Kyoto meant. The roads were rough and bad, and ordinary people had to walk every step of the way, whether the distance were one hundred or several hundred miles. Indeed, in those days it was as great an undertaking to go up to the capital as it is for a Japanese to make a voyage to Europe now. So the wife was very anxious while she helped her husband get ready for the long journey, knowing what an arduous task lay before him. Vainly she wished that she could accompany him, but the distance was too great for the mother and child to go, and besides that, it was the wife's duty to take care of the home.

All was ready at last, and the husband stood in the porch with his little family round him.

"Do not be anxious, I will come back soon," said the man. "While I am away take care of everything, and especially of our little daughter."

"Yes, we shall be all right—but you—you must take care of yourself and delay not a day in coming back to us," said the wife, while the tears fell like rain from her eyes.

The little girl was the only one to smile, for she was ignorant of the sorrow of parting, and did not know that going to the capital was at all different from walking to the next village, which her father did very often. She ran to his side, and caught hold of his long sleeve to keep him a moment.

"Father, I will be very good while I am waiting for you to come back, so please bring me a present."

As the father turned to take a last look at his weeping wife and smiling, eager child, he felt as if some one were pulling him back by the hair, so hard was it for him to leave them behind, for they had never been separated before. But he knew that he must go, for the call was imperative. With a great effort he ceased to think, and resolutely turning away he went quickly down the little garden and out through the gate. His wife, catching up the child in her arms, ran as far as the gate, and watched him as he went down the road between the pines till he was lost in the haze of the distance and all she could see was his quaint peaked hat, and at last that vanished too.

"Now father has gone, you and I must take care of everything till he comes back," said the mother, as she made her way back to the house.

"Yes, I will be very good," said the child, nodding her head, "and when father comes home please tell him how good I have been, and then perhaps he will give me a present."

"Father is sure to bring you something that you want very much. I know, for I asked him to bring you a doll. You must think of father every day, and pray for a safe journey till he comes back."

"O, yes, when he comes home again how happy I shall be," said the child, clapping her hands, and her face growing bright with joy at the glad thought. It seemed to the mother as she looked at the child's face that her love for her grew deeper and deeper.

Then she set to work to make the winter clothes for the three of them. She set up her simple wooden spinning-wheel and spun the thread before she began to weave the stuffs. In the intervals of her work she directed the little girl's games and taught her to read the old stories of her country. Thus did the wife find consolation in work during the lonely days of her husband's absence. While the time was thus slipping quickly by in the quiet home, the husband finished his business and returned. It would have been difficult for anyone who did not know the man well to recognize him. He had traveled day after day, exposed to all weathers, for about a month altogether, and was sunburnt to bronze, but his fond wife and child knew him at a glance, and flew to meet him from either side, each catching hold of one of his sleeves in their eager greeting. Both the man and his wife rejoiced to find each other well. It seemed a very long time to all till—the mother and child helping—his straw sandals were untied, his large umbrella hat taken off, and he was again in their midst in the old familiar sitting-room that had been so empty while he was away.

As soon as they had sat down on the white mats, the father opened a bamboo basket that he had brought in with him, and took out a beautiful doll and a lacquer box full of cakes.

"Here," he said to the little girl, "is a present for you. It is a prize for taking care of mother and the house so well while I was away."

"Thank you," said the child, as she bowed her head to the ground, and then put out her hand just like a little maple leaf with its eager wide-spread fingers to take the doll and the box, both of which, coming from the capital, were prettier than anything she had ever seen. No words can tell how delighted the little girl was—her face seemed as if it would melt with joy, and she had no eyes and no thought for anything else.

Again the husband dived into the basket, and brought out this time a square wooden box, carefully tied up with red and white string, and handing it to his wife, said:

"And this is for you."

The wife took the box, and opening it carefully took out a metal disk with a handle attached. One side was bright and shining like a crystal, and the other was covered with raised figures of pine-trees and storks, which had been carved out of its smooth surface in lifelike reality. Never had she seen such a thing in her life, for she had been born and bred in the rural province of Echigo. She gazed into the shining disk, and looking up with surprise and wonder pictured on her face, she said:

"I see somebody looking at me in this round thing! What is it that you have given me?"

The husband laughed and said:

"Why, it is your own face that you see. What I have brought you is called a mirror, and whoever looks into its clear surface can see their own form reflected there. Although there are none to be found in this out of the way place, yet they have been in use in the capital from the most ancient times. There the mirror is considered a very necessary requisite for a woman to possess. There is an old proverb that 'As the sword is the soul of a samurai, so is the mirror the soul of a woman,' and according to popular tradition, a woman's mirror is an index to her own heart—if she keeps it bright and clear, so is her heart pure and good. It is also one of the treasures that form the insignia of the Emperor. So you must lay great store by your mirror, and use it carefully."

The wife listened to all her husband told her, and was pleased at learning so much that was new to her. She was still more pleased at the precious gift—his token of remembrance while he had been away.

"If the mirror represents my soul, I shall certainly treasure it as a valuable possession, and never will I use it carelessly." Saying so, she lifted it as high as her forehead, in grateful acknowledgment of the gift, and then shut it up in its box and put it away.

The wife saw that her husband was very tired, and set about serving the evening meal and making everything as comfortable as she could for him. It seemed to the little family as if they had not known what true happiness was before, so glad were they to be together again, and this evening the father had much to tell of his journey and of all he had seen at the great capital.

Time passed away in the peaceful home, and the parents saw their fondest hopes realized as their daughter grew from childhood into a beautiful girl of sixteen. As a gem of priceless value is held in its proud owner's hand, so had they reared her with unceasing love and care: and now their pains were more than doubly rewarded. What a comfort she was to her mother as she went about the house taking her part in the housekeeping, and how proud her father was of her, for she daily reminded him of her mother when he had first married her.

But, alas! in this world nothing lasts forever. Even the moon is not always perfect in shape, but loses its roundness with time, and flowers bloom and then fade. So at last the happiness of this family was broken up by a great sorrow. The good and gentle wife and mother was one day taken ill.

In the first days of her illness the father and daughter thought that it was only a cold, and were not particularly anxious. But the days went by and still the mother did not get better; she only grew worse, and the doctor was puzzled, for in spite of all he did the poor woman grew weaker day by day. The father and daughter were stricken with grief, and day or night the girl never left her mother's side. But in spite of all their efforts the woman's life was not to be saved.

One day as the girl sat near her mother's bed, trying to hide with a cheery smile the gnawing trouble at her heart, the mother roused herself and taking her daughter's hand, gazed earnestly and lovingly into her eyes. Her breath was labored and she spoke with difficulty:

"My daughter. I am sure that nothing can save me now. When I am dead, promise me to take care of your dear father and to try to be a good and dutiful woman."

"Oh, mother," said the girl as the tears rushed to her eyes, "you must not say such things. All you have to do is to make haste and get well—that will bring the greatest happiness to father and myself."

"Yes, I know, and it is a comfort to me in my last days to know how greatly you long for me to get better, but it is not to be. Do not look so sorrowful, for it was so ordained in my previous state of existence that I should die in this life just at this time; knowing this, I am quite resigned to my fate. And now I have something to give you whereby to remember me when I am gone."

Putting her hand out, she took from the side of the pillow a square wooden box tied up with a silken cord and tassels. Undoing this very carefully, she took out of the box the mirror that her husband had given her years ago.

"When you were still a little child your father went up to the capital and brought me back as a present this treasure; it is called a mirror. This I give you before I die. If, after I have ceased to be in this life, you are lonely and long to see me sometimes, then take out this mirror and in the clear and shining surface you will always see me—so will you be able to meet with me often and tell me all your heart; and though I shall not be able to speak, I shall understand and sympathize with you, whatever may happen to you in the future." With these words the dying woman handed the mirror to her daughter. The mind of the good mother seemed to be now at rest, and sinking back without another word her spirit passed quietly away that day.

The bereaved father and daughter were wild with grief, and they abandoned themselves to their bitter sorrow. They felt it to be impossible to take leave of the loved woman who till now had filled their whole lives and to commit her body to the earth. But this frantic burst of grief passed, and then they took possession of their own hearts again, crushed though they were in resignation. In spite of this the daughter's life seemed to her desolate. Her love for her dead mother did not grow less with time, and so keen was her remembrance, that everything in daily life, even the falling of the rain and the blowing of the wind, reminded her of her mother's death and of all that they had loved and shared together. One day when her father was out, and she was fulfilling her household duties alone, her loneliness and sorrow seemed more than she could bear. She threw herself down in her mother's room and wept as if her heart would break. Poor child, she longed just for one glimpse of the loved face, one sound of the voice calling her pet name, or for one moment's forgetfulness of the aching void in her heart. Suddenly she sat up. Her mother's last words had rung through her memory hitherto dulled by grief.

"Oh! my mother told me when she gave me the mirror as a parting gift, that whenever I looked into it I should be able to meet her—to see her. I had nearly forgotten her last words—how stupid I am; I will get the mirror now and see if it can possibly be true!"

She dried her eyes quickly, and going to the cupboard took out the box that contained the mirror, her heart beating with expectation as she lifted the mirror out and gazed into its smooth face. Behold, her mother's words were true! In the round mirror before her she saw her mother's face; but, oh, the joyful surprise! It was not her mother thin and wasted by illness, but the young and beautiful woman as she remembered her far back in the days of her own earliest childhood. It seemed to the girl that the face in the mirror must soon speak, almost that she heard the voice of her mother telling her again to grow up a good woman and a dutiful daughter, so earnestly did the eyes in the mirror look back into her own.

"It is certainly my mother's soul that I see. She knows how miserable I am without her and she has come to comfort me. Whenever I long to see her she will meet me here; how grateful I ought to be!"

And from this time the weight of sorrow was greatly lightened for her young heart. Every morning, to gather strength for the day's duties before her, and every evening, for consolation before she lay down to rest, did the young girl take out the mirror and gaze at the reflection which in the simplicity of her innocent heart she believed to be her mother's soul. Daily she grew in the likeness of her dead mother's character, and was gentle and kind to all, and a dutiful daughter to her father.

A year spent in mourning had thus passed away in the little household, when, by the advice of his relations, the man married again, and the daughter now found herself under the authority of a step-mother. It was a trying position; but her days spent in the recollection of her own beloved mother, and of trying to be what that mother would wish her to be, had made the young girl docile and patient, and she now determined to be filial and dutiful to her father's wife, in all respects. Everything went on apparently smoothly in the family for some time under the new regime; there were no winds or waves of discord to ruffle the surface of every-day life, and the father was content.

But it is a woman's danger to be petty and mean, and step-mothers are proverbial all the world over, and this one's heart was not as her first smiles were. As the days and weeks grew into months, the step-mother began to treat the motherless girl unkindly and to try and come between the father and child. Sometimes she went to her husband and complained of her step-daughter's behavior, but the father knowing that this was to be expected, took no notice of her ill-natured complaints. Instead of lessening his affection for his daughter, as the woman desired, her grumblings only made him think of her the more. The woman soon saw that he began to show more concern for his lonely child than before. This did not please her at all, and she began to turn over in her mind how she could, by some means or other, drive her step-child out of the house. So crooked did the woman's heart become.

She watched the girl carefully, and one day peeping into her room in the early morning, she thought she discovered a grave enough sin of which to accuse the child to her father. The woman herself was a little frightened too at what she had seen.

So she went at once to her husband, and wiping away some false tears she said in a sad voice:

"Please give me permission to leave you today."

The man was completely taken by surprise at the suddenness of her request, and wondered whatever was the matter.

"Do you find it so disagreeable," he asked, "in my house, that you can stay no longer?"

"No! no! it has nothing to do with you—even in my dreams I have never thought that I wished to leave your side; but if I go on living here I am in danger of losing my life, so I think it best for all concerned that you should allow me to go home!"

And the woman began to weep afresh. Her husband, distressed to see her so unhappy, and thinking that he could not have heard aright, said:

"Tell me what you mean! How is your life in danger here?"

"I will tell you since you ask me. Your daughter dislikes me as her step-mother. For some time past she has shut herself up in her room morning and evening, and looking in as I pass by, I am convinced that she has made an image of me and is trying to kill me by magic art, cursing me daily. It is not safe for me to stay here, such being the case; indeed, indeed, I must go away, we cannot live under the same roof any more."

The husband listened to the dreadful tale, but he could not believe his gentle daughter guilty of such an evil act. He knew that by popular superstition people believed that one person could cause the gradual death of another by making an image of the hated one and cursing it daily; but where had his young daughter learned such knowledge?—the thing was impossible. Yet he remembered having noticed that his daughter stayed much in her room of late and kept herself away from every one, even when visitors came to the house. Putting this fact together with his wife's alarm, he thought that there might be something to account for the strange story.

His heart was torn between doubting his wife and trusting his child, and he knew not what to do. He decided to go at once to his daughter and try to find out the truth. Comforting his wife and assuring her that her fears were groundless, he glided quietly to his daughter's room.

The girl had for a long time past been very unhappy. She had tried by amiability and obedience to show her goodwill and to mollify the new wife, and to break down that wall of prejudice and misunderstanding that she knew generally stood between step-parents and their step-children. But she soon found that her efforts were in vain. The step-mother never trusted her, and seemed to misinterpret all her actions, and the poor child knew very well that she often carried unkind and untrue tales to her father. She could not help comparing her present unhappy condition with the time when her own mother was alive only a little more than a year ago—so great a change in this short time! Morning and evening she wept over the remembrance. Whenever she could she went to her room, and sliding the screens to, took out the mirror and gazed, as she thought, at her mother's face. It was the only comfort that she had in these wretched days.

Her father found her occupied in this way. Pushing aside the fusama, he saw her bending over something or other very intently. Looking over her shoulder, to see who was entering her room, the girl was surprised to see her father, for he generally sent for her when he wished to speak to her. She was also confused at being found looking at the mirror, for she had never told any one of her mother's last promise, but had kept it as the sacred secret of her heart. So before turning to her father she slipped the mirror into her long sleeve. Her father noting her confusion, and her act of hiding something, said in a severe manner:

"Daughter, what are you doing here? And what is that that you have hidden in your sleeve?"

The girl was frightened by her father's severity. Never had he spoken to her in such a tone. Her confusion changed to apprehension, her color from scarlet to white. She sat dumb and shamefaced, unable to reply.

Appearances were certainly against her; the young girl looked guilty, and the father thinking that perhaps after all what his wife had told him was true, spoke angrily:

"Then, is it really true that you are daily cursing your step-mother and praying for her death? Have you forgotten what I told you, that although she is your step-mother you must be obedient and loyal to her? What evil spirit has taken possession of your heart that you should be so wicked? You have certainly changed, my daughter! What has made you so disobedient and unfaithful?"

And the father's eyes filled with sudden tears to think that he should have to upbraid his daughter in this way.

She on her part did not know what he meant, for she had never heard of the superstition that by praying over an image it is possible to cause the death of a hated person. But she saw that she must speak and clear herself somehow. She loved her father dearly, and could not bear the idea of his anger. She put out her hand on his knee deprecatingly:

"Father! father! do not say such dreadful things to me. I am still your obedient child. Indeed, I am. However stupid I may be, I should never be able to curse any one who belonged to you, much less pray for the death of one you love. Surely some one has been telling you lies, and you are dazed, and you know not what you say—or some evil spirit has taken possession of YOUR heart. As for me I do not know—no, not so much as a dew-drop, of the evil thing of which you accuse me."

But the father remembered that she had hidden something away when he first entered the room, and even this earnest protest did not satisfy him. He wished to clear up his doubts once for all.

"Then why are you always alone in your room these days? And tell me what is that that you have hidden in your sleeve—show it to me at once."

Then the daughter, though shy of confessing how she had cherished her mother's memory, saw that she must tell her father all in order to clear herself. So she slipped the mirror out from her long sleeve and laid it before him.

"This," she said, "is what you saw me looking at just now."

"Why," he said in great surprise, "this is the mirror that I brought as a gift to your mother when I went up to the capital many years ago! And so you have kept it all this time? Now, why do you spend so much of your time before this mirror?" Then she told him of her mother's last words, and of how she had promised to meet her child whenever she looked into the glass. But still the father could not understand the simplicity of his daughter's character in not knowing that what she saw reflected in the mirror was in reality her own face, and not that of her mother.

"What do you mean?" he asked. "I do not understand how you can meet the soul of your lost mother by looking in this mirror?" "It is indeed true," said the girl: "and if you don't believe what I say, look for yourself," and she placed the mirror before her. There, looking back from the smooth metal disk, was her own sweet face. She pointed to the reflection seriously:

"Do you doubt me still?" she asked earnestly, looking up into his face.

With an exclamation of sudden understanding the father smote his two hands together.

"How stupid I am! At last I understand. Your face is as like your mother's as the two sides of a melon—thus you have looked at the reflection of your face ail this time, thinking that you were brought face to face with your lost mother! You are truly a faithful child. It seems at first a stupid thing to have done, but it is not really so, It shows how deep has been your filial piety, and how innocent your heart. Living in constant remembrance of your lost mother has helped you to grow like her in character. How clever it was of her to tell you to do this. I admire and respect you, my daughter, and I am ashamed to think that for one instant I believed your suspicious step-mother's story and suspected you of evil, and came with the intention of scolding you severely, while all this time you have been so true and good. Before you I have no countenance left, and I beg you to forgive me."

And here the father wept. He thought of how lonely the poor girl must have been, and of all that she must have suffered under her step-mother's treatment. His daughter steadfastly keeping her faith and simplicity in the midst of such adverse circumstances—bearing all her troubles with so much patience and amiability—made him compare her to the lotus which rears its blossom of dazzling beauty out of the slime and mud of the moats and ponds, fitting emblem of a heart which keeps itself unsullied while passing through the world. The step-mother, anxious to know what would happen, had all this while been standing outside the room. She had grown interested, and had gradually pushed the sliding screen back till she could see all that went on. At this moment she suddenly entered the room, and dropping to the mats, she bowed her head over her outspread hands before her step-daughter.

"I am ashamed! I am ashamed!" she exclaimed in broken tones. "I did not know what a filial child you were. Through no fault of yours, but with a step-mother's jealous heart, I have disliked you all the time. Hating you so much myself, it was but natural that I should think you reciprocated the feeling, and thus when I saw you retire so often to your room I followed you, and when I saw you gaze daily into the mirror for long intervals, I concluded that you had found out how I disliked you, and that you were out of revenge trying to take my life by magic art. As long as I live I shall never forget the wrong I have done you in so misjudging you, and in causing your father to suspect you. From this day I throw away my old and wicked heart, and in its place I put a new one, clean and full of repentance. I shall think of you as a child that I have borne myself. I shall love and cherish you with all my heart, and thus try to make up for all the unhappiness I have caused you. Therefore, please throw into the water all that has gone before, and give me, I beg of you, some of the filial love that you have hitherto given to your own lost mother."

Thus did the unkind step-mother humble herself and ask forgiveness of the girl she had so wronged. Such was the sweetness of the girl's disposition that she willingly forgave her step-mother, and never bore a moment's resentment or malice towards her afterwards. The father saw by his wife's face that she was truly sorry for the past, and was greatly relieved to see the terrible misunderstanding wiped out of remembrance by both the wrong-doer and the wronged.

From this time on, the three lived together as happily as fish in water. No such trouble ever darkened the home again, and the young girl gradually forgot that year of unhappiness in the tender love and care that her step-mother now bestowed on her. Her patience and goodness were rewarded at last.

The Edo period and Japan's fables provide a model for a sustainable Japan

Cover of Japanese Fairy Tale Series Number 1 Momotaro published by T. Hasegawa in 1886.

Statue de Momotarō et ses compagnons, à Okayama

MOMOTARO, OR THE STORY OF THE SON OF A PEACH.

Long, long ago there lived, an old man and an old woman; they were peasants, and had to work hard to earn their daily rice. The old man used to go and cut grass for the farmers around, and while he was gone the old woman, his wife, did the work of the house and worked in their own little rice field.

One day the old man went to the hills as usual to cut grass and the old woman took some clothes to the river to wash.

It was nearly summer, and the country was very beautiful to see in its fresh greenness as the two old people went on their way to work. The grass on the banks of the river looked like emerald velvet, and the pussy willows along the edge of the water were shaking out their soft tassels.

The breezes blew and ruffled the smooth surface of the water into wavelets, and passing on touched the cheeks of the old couple who, for some reason they could not explain, felt very happy that morning.

The old woman at last found a nice spot by the river bank and put her basket down. Then she set to work to wash the clothes; she took them one by one out of the basket and washed them in the river and rubbed them on the stones. The water was as clear as crystal, and she could see the tiny fish swimming to and fro, and the pebbles at the bottom.

As she was busy washing her clothes a great peach came bumping down the stream. The old woman looked up from her work and saw this large peach. She was sixty years of age, yet in all her life she had never seen such a big peach as this.

"How delicious that peach must be!" she said to herself. "I must certainly get it and take it home to my old man."

She stretched out her arm to try and get it, but it was quite out of her reach. She looked about for a stick, but there was not one to be seen, and if she went to look for one she would lose the peach.

Stopping a moment to think what she would do, she remembered an old charm-verse. Now she began to clap her hands to keep time to the rolling of the peach down stream, and while she clapped she sang this song:

"Distant water is bitter,
The near water is sweet;
Pass by the distant water
And come into the sweet."

Strange to say, as soon as she began to repeat this little song the peach began to come nearer and nearer the bank where the old woman was standing, till at last it stopped just in front of her so that she was able to take it up in her hands. The old woman was delighted. She could not go on with her work, so happy and excited was she, so she put all the clothes back in her bamboo basket, and with the basket on her back and the peach in her hand she hurried homewards.

It seemed a very long time to her to wait till her husband returned. The old man at last came back as the sun was setting, with a big bundle of grass on his back—so big that he was almost hidden and she could hardly see him. He seemed very tired and used the scythe for a walking stick, leaning on it as he walked along.

As soon as the old woman saw him she called out:

"O Fii San! (old man) I have been waiting for you to come home for such a long time to-day!"

47

"What is the matter? Why are you so impatient?" asked the old man, wondering at her unusual eagerness. "Has anything happened while I have been away?"

"Oh, no!" answered the old woman, "nothing has happened, only I have found a nice present for you!"

"That is good," said the old man. He then washed his feet in a basin of water and stepped up to the veranda.

The old woman now ran into the little room and brought out from the cupboard the big peach. It felt even heavier than before. She held it up to him, saying:

"Just look at this! Did you ever see such a large peach in all your life?"

When the old man looked at the peach he was greatly astonished and said:

"This is indeed the largest peach I have ever seen! Wherever did you buy it?"

"I did not buy it," answered the old woman. "I found it in the river where I was washing." And she told him the whole story.

"I am very glad that you have found it. Let us eat it now, for I am hungry," said the O Fii San.

He brought out the kitchen knife, and, placing the peach on a board, was about to cut it when, wonderful to tell, the peach split in two of itself and a clear voice said:

"Wait a bit, old man!" and out stepped a beautiful little child.

The old man and his wife were both so astonished at what they saw that they fell to the ground. The child spoke again:

"Don't be afraid. I am no demon or fairy. I will tell you the truth. Heaven has had compassion on you. Every day and every night you have lamented that you had no child. Your cry has been heard and I am sent to be the son of your old age!"

On hearing this the old man and his wife were very happy. They had cried night and day for sorrow at having no child to help them in their lonely old age, and now that their prayer was answered they were so lost with joy that they did not know where to put their hands or their feet. First the old man took the child up in his arms, and then the old woman did the same; and they named him MOMOTARO, OR SON OF A PEACH, because he had come out of a peach.

The years passed quickly by and the child grew to be fifteen years of age. He was taller and far stronger than any other boys of his own age, he had a handsome face and a heart full of courage, and he was very wise for his years. The old couple's pleasure was very great when they looked at him, for he was just what they thought a hero ought to be like.

One day Momotaro came to his foster-father and said solemnly:

"Father, by a strange chance we have become father and son. Your goodness to me has been higher than the mountain grasses which it was your daily work to cut, and deeper than the river where my mother washes the clothes. I do not know how to thank you enough."

"Why," answered the old man, "it is a matter of course that a father should bring up his son. When you are older it will be your turn to take care of us, so after all there will be no profit or loss between us—all will be equal. Indeed, I am rather surprised that you should thank me in this way!" and the old man looked bothered.

"I hope you will be patient with me," said Momotaro; "but before I begin to pay back your goodness to me I have a request to make which I hope you will grant me above everything else."

"I will let you do whatever you wish, for you are quite different to all other boys!"

"Then let me go away at once!"

"What do you say? Do you wish to leave your old father and mother and go away from your old home?"

"I will surely come back again, if you let me go now!"

"Where are you going?"

"You must think it strange that I want to go away," said Momotaro, "because I have not yet told you my reason. Far away from here to the northeast of Japan there is an island in the sea. This island is the stronghold of a band of devils. I have often heard how they invade this land, kill and rob the people, and carry off all they can find. They are not only very wicked but they are disloyal to our Emperor and disobey his laws. They are also cannibals, for they kill and eat some of the poor people who are so unfortunate as to fall into their hands. These devils are very hateful beings. I must go and conquer them and bring back all the plunder of which they have robbed this land. It is for this reason that I want to go away for a short time!"

The old man was much surprised at hearing all this from a mere boy of fifteen. He thought it best to let the boy go. He was strong and fearless, and besides all this, the old man knew he was no common child, for he had been sent to them as a gift from Heaven, and he felt quite sure that the devils would be powerless to harm him.

"All you say is very interesting, Momotaro," said the old man. "I will not hinder you in your determination. You may go if you wish. Go to the island as soon as ever you like and destroy the demons and bring peace to the land."

"Thank you, for all your kindness," said Momotaro, who began to get ready to go that very day. He was full of courage and did not know what fear was.

The old man and woman at once set to work to pound rice in the kitchen mortar to make cakes for Momotaro to take with him on his journey.

At last the cakes were made and Momotaro was ready to start on his long journey.

Parting is always sad. So it was now. The eyes of the two old people were filled with tears and their voices trembled as they said:

"Go with all care and speed. We expect you back victorious!"

Momotaro was very sorry to leave his old parents (though he knew he was coming back as soon as he could), for he thought of how lonely they would be while he was away. But he said "Good-by!" quite bravely.

"I am going now. Take good care of yourselves while I am away. Good-by!" And he stepped quickly out of the house. In silence the eyes of Momotaro and his parents met in farewell.

Momotaro now hurried on his way till it was midday. He began to feel hungry, so he opened his bag and took out one of the rice-cakes and sat down under a tree by the side of the road to eat it. While he was thus having his lunch a dog almost as large as a colt came running out from the high grass. He made straight for Momotaro, and showing his teeth, said in a fierce way:

"You are a rude man to pass my field without asking permission first. If you leave me all the cakes you have in your bag you may go; otherwise I will bite you till I kill you!"

Momotaro only laughed scornfully:

"What is that you are saying? Do you know who I am? I am Momotaro, and I am on my way to subdue the devils in their island stronghold in the northeast of Japan. If you try to stop me on my way there I will cut you in two from the head downwards!"

The dog's manner at once changed. His tail dropped between his legs, and coming near he bowed so low that his forehead touched the ground.

"What do I hear? The name of Momotaro? Are you indeed Momotaro? I have often heard of your great strength. Not knowing who you were I have behaved in a very stupid way. Will you please pardon my rudeness? Are you indeed on your way to invade the Island of Devils? If you will take such a rude fellow with you as one of your followers, I shall be very grateful to you."

"I think I can take you with me if you wish to go," said Momotaro.

"Thank you!" said the dog. "By the way, I am very very hungry. Will you give me one of the cakes you are carrying?"

"This is the best kind of cake there is in Japan," said Momotaro. "I cannot spare you a whole one; I will give you half of one."

"Thank you very much," said the dog, taking the piece thrown to him.

Then Momotaro got up and the dog followed. For a long time they walked over the hills and through the valleys. As they were going along an animal came down from a tree a little ahead of them. The creature soon came up to Momotaro and said:

"Good morning, Momotaro! You are welcome in this part of the country. Will you allow me to go with you?"

The dog answered jealously:

"Momotaro already has a dog to accompany him. Of what use is a monkey like you in battle? We are on our way to fight the devils! Get away!"

The dog and the monkey began to quarrel and bite, for these two animals always hate each other.

"Now, don't quarrel!" said Momotaro, putting himself between them. "Wait a moment, dog!"

"It is not at all dignified for you to have such a creature as that following you!" said the dog.

"What do you know about it?" asked Momotaro; and pushing aside the dog, he spoke to the monkey:

"Who are you?"

"I am a monkey living in these hills," replied the monkey. "I heard of your expedition to the Island of Devils, and I have come to go with you. Nothing will please me more than to follow you!"

"Do you really wish to go to the Island of Devils and fight with me?"

"Yes, sir," replied the monkey.

"I admire your courage," said Momotaro. "Here is a piece of one of my fine rice-cakes. Come along!"

So the monkey joined Momotaro. The dog and the monkey did not get on well together. They were always snapping at each other as they went along, and always wanting to have a fight. This made Momotaro very cross, and at last he sent the dog on ahead with a flag and put the monkey behind with a sword, and he placed himself between them with a war-fan, which is made of iron.

By and by they came to a large field. Here a bird flew down and alighted on the ground just in front of the little party. It was the most beautiful bird Momotaro had ever seen. On its body were five different robes of feathers and its head was covered with a scarlet cap.

The dog at once ran at the bird and tried to seize and kill it. But the bird struck out its spurs and flew at the dog's tail, and the fight went hard with both.

Momotaro, as he looked on, could not help admiring the bird; it showed so much spirit in the fight. It would certainly make a good fighter.

Momotaro went up to the two combatants, and holding the dog back, said to the bird:

"You rascal! you are hindering my journey. Surrender at once, and I will take you with me. If you don't I will set this dog to bite your head off!"

Then the bird surrendered at once, and begged to be taken into Momotaro's company.

"I do not know what excuse to offer for quarreling with the dog, your servant, but I did not see you. I am a miserable bird called a pheasant. It is very generous of you to pardon my rudeness and to take me with you. Please allow me to follow you behind the dog and the monkey!"

"I congratulate you on surrendering so soon," said Momotaro, smiling. "Come and join us in our raid on the devils."

"Are you going to take this bird with you also?" asked the dog, interrupting.

"Why do you ask such an unnecessary question? Didn't you hear what I said? I take the bird with me because I wish to!"

"Humph!" said the dog.

Then Momotaro stood and gave this order:

"Now all of you must listen to me. The first thing necessary in an army is harmony. It is a wise saying which says that 'Advantage on earth is better than advantage in Heaven!' Union amongst ourselves is better than any earthly gain. When we are not at peace amongst ourselves it is no easy thing to subdue an enemy. From now, you three, the dog, the monkey and the pheasant, must be friends with one mind. The one who first begins a quarrel will be discharged on the spot!"

All the three promised not to quarrel. The pheasant was now made a member of Momotaro's suite, and received half a cake.

Momotaro's influence was so great that the three became good friends, and hurried onwards with him as their leader.

Hurrying on day after day they at last came out upon the shore of the North-Eastern Sea. There was nothing to be seen as far as the horizon—not a sign of any island. All that broke the stillness was the rolling of the waves upon the shore.

Now, the dog and the monkey and the pheasant had come very bravely all the way through the long valleys and over the hills, but they had never seen the sea before, and for the first time since they set out they were bewildered and gazed at each other in silence. How were they to cross the water and get to the Island of Devils?

Momotaro soon saw that they were daunted by the sight of the sea, and to try them he spoke loudly and roughly:

"Why do you hesitate? Are you afraid of the sea? Oh! what cowards you are! It is impossible to take such weak creatures as you with me to fight the demons. It will be far better for me to go alone. I discharge you all at once!"

The three animals were taken aback at this sharp reproof, and clung to Momotaro's sleeve, begging him not to send them away.

"Please, Momotaro!" said the dog.

"We have come thus far!" said the monkey.

"It is inhuman to leave us here!" said the pheasant.

"We are not at all afraid of the sea," said the monkey again.

"Please do take us with you," said the pheasant.

"Do please," said the dog.

They had now gained a little courage, so Momotaro said:

"Well, then, I will take you with me, but be careful!"

Momotaro now got a small ship, and they all got on board. The wind and weather were fair, and the ship went like an arrow over the sea. It was the first time they had ever been on the water, and so at first the dog, the monkey and the pheasant were frightened at the waves and the rolling of the vessel, but by degrees they grew accustomed to the water and were quite happy again. Every day they paced the deck of their little ship, eagerly looking out for the demons' island.

When they grew tired of this, they told each other stories of all their exploits of which they were proud, and then played games together; and Momotaro found much to amuse him in listening to the three animals and watching their antics, and in this way he forgot that the way was long and that he was tired of the voyage and of doing nothing. He longed to be at work killing the monsters who had done so much harm in his country.

As the wind blew in their favor and they met no storms the ship made a quick voyage, and one day when the sun was shining brightly a sight of land rewarded the four watchers at the bow.

Momotaro knew at once that what they saw was the devils' stronghold. On the top of the precipitous shore, looking out to sea, was a large castle. Now that his enterprise was close at hand, he was deep in thought with his head leaning on his hands, wondering how he should begin the attack. His three followers watched him, waiting for orders. At last he called to the pheasant:

"It is a great advantage for us to have you with us." said Momotaro to the bird, "for you have good wings. Fly at once to the castle and engage the demons to fight. We will follow you."

The pheasant at once obeyed. He flew off from the ship beating the air gladly with his wings. The bird soon reached the island and took up his position on the roof in the middle of the castle, calling out loudly:

"All you devils listen to me! The great Japanese general Momotaro has come to fight you and to take your stronghold from you. If you wish to save your lives surrender at once, and in token of your submission you must break off the horns that grow on your forehead. If you do not surrender at once, but make up your mind to fight, we, the pheasant, the dog and the monkey, will kill you all by biting and tearing you to death!"

The horned demons looking up and only seeing a pheasant, laughed and said:

"A wild pheasant, indeed! It is ridiculous to hear such words from a mean thing like you. Wait till you get a blow from one of our iron bars!"

Very angry, indeed, were the devils. They shook their horns and their shocks of red hair fiercely, and rushed to put on tiger skin trousers to make themselves look more terrible. They then brought out great iron bars and ran to where the pheasant perched over their heads, and tried to knock him down. The pheasant flew to one side to escape the blow, and then attacked the head of first one and then another demon. He flew round and round them, beating the air with his wings so fiercely and ceaselessly, that the devils began to wonder whether they had to fight one or many more birds.

In the meantime, Momotaro had brought his ship to land. As they had approached, he saw that the shore was like a precipice, and that the large castle was surrounded by high walls and large iron gates and was strongly fortified.

Momotaro landed, and with the hope of finding some way of entrance, walked up the path towards the top, followed by the monkey and the dog. They soon came upon two beautiful damsels washing clothes in a stream. Momotaro saw that the clothes were blood-stained, and that as the two maidens washed, the tears were falling fast down their cheeks. He stopped and spoke to them:

"Who are you, and why do you weep?"

"We are captives of the Demon King. We were carried away from our homes to this island, and though we are the daughters of Daimios (Lords), we are obliged to be his servants, and one day he will kill us"—and the maidens held up the blood-stained clothes—"and eat us, and there is no one to help us!"

And their tears burst out afresh at this horrible thought.

"I will rescue you," said Momotaro. "Do not weep any more, only show me how I may get into the castle."

Then the two ladies led the way and showed Momotaro a little back door in the lowest part of the castle wall—so small that Momotaro could hardly crawl in.

The pheasant, who was all this time fighting hard, saw Momotaro and his little band rush in at the back.

Momotaro's onslaught was so furious that the devils could not stand against him. At first their foe had been a single bird, the pheasant, but now that Momotaro and the dog and the monkey had arrived they were bewildered, for the four enemies fought like a hundred, so strong were they. Some of the devils fell off the parapet of the castle and were dashed to pieces on the rocks beneath; others fell into the sea and were drowned; many were beaten to death by the three animals.

The chief of the devils at last was the only one left. He made up his mind to surrender, for he knew that his enemy was stronger than mortal man.

He came up humbly to Momotaro and threw down his iron bar, and kneeling down at the victor's feet he broke off the horns on his head in token of submission, for they were the sign of his strength and power.

"I am afraid of you," he said meekly. "I cannot stand against you. I will give you all the treasure hidden in this castle if you will spare my life!"

Momotaro laughed.

"It is not like you, big devil, to beg for mercy, is it? I cannot spare your wicked life, however much you beg, for you have killed and tortured many people and robbed our country for many years."

Then Momotaro tied the devil chief up and gave him into the monkey's charge. Having done this, he went into all the rooms of the castle and set the prisoners free and gathered together all the treasure he found.

The dog and the pheasant carried home the plunder, and thus Momotaro returned triumphantly to his home, taking with him the devil chief as a captive.

The two poor damsels, daughters of Daimios, and others whom the wicked demon had carried off to be his slaves, were taken safely to their own homes and delivered to their parents.

The whole country made a hero of Momotaro on his triumphant return, and rejoiced that the country was now freed from the robber devils who had been a terror of the land for a long time.

The old couple's joy was greater than ever, and the treasure Momotaro had brought home with him enabled them to live in peace and plenty to the end of their days.

THE WHITE HARE AND THE CROCODILES

Long, long ago, when all the animals could talk, there lived in the province of Inaba in Japan, a little white hare. His home was on the island of Oki, and just across the sea was the mainland of Inaba.

Now the hare wanted very much to cross over to Inaba. Day after day he would go out and sit on the shore and look longingly over the water in the direction of Inaba, and day after day he hoped to find some way of getting across.

One day as usual, the hare was standing on the beach, looking towards the mainland across the water, when he saw a great crocodile swimming near the island.

"This is very lucky!" thought the hare. "Now I shall be able to get my wish. I will ask the crocodile to carry me across the sea!"

But he was doubtful whether the crocodile would consent to do what wanted. So he thought instead of asking a favor he would try to get what he wanted by a trick.

So with a loud voice he called to the crocodile, and said:

"Oh, Mr. Crocodile, isn't it a lovely day?"

The crocodile, who had come out all by itself that day to enjoy the bright sunshine, was just beginning to feel a bit lonely when the hare's cheerful greeting broke the silence. The crocodile swam nearer the shore, very pleased to hear some one speak.

"I wonder who it was that spoke to me just now! Was it you, Mr. Hare? You must be very lonely all by yourself!"

"Oh, no, I am not at all lonely," said the hare, "but as it was such a fine day I came out here to enjoy myself. Won't you stop and play with me a little while?"

The crocodile came out of the sea and sat on the shore, and the two played together for some time. Then the hare said:

"Mr. Crocodile, you live in the sea and I live on this island, and we do not often meet, so I know very little about you. Tell me, do you think the number of your company is greater than mine?"

"Of course, there are more crocodiles than hares," answered the crocodile. "Can you not see that for yourself? You live on this small island, while I live in the sea, which spreads through all parts of the world, so if I call together all the crocodiles who dwell in the sea you hares will be as nothing compared to us!" The crocodile was very conceited.

The hare, who meant to play a trick on the crocodile, said:

"Do you think it possible for you to call up enough crocodiles to form a line from this island across the sea to Inaba?"

The crocodile thought for a moment and then answered:

"Of course, it is possible."

"Then do try," said the artful hare, "and I will count the number from here!"

The crocodile, who was very simple-minded, and who hadn't the least idea that the hare intended to play a trick on him, agreed to do what the hare asked, and said:

"Wait a little while I go back into the sea and call my company together!"

The crocodile plunged into the sea and was gone for some time. The hare, meanwhile, waited patiently on the shore. At last the crocodile appeared, bringing with him a large number of other crocodiles.

"Look, Mr. Hare!" said the crocodile, "it is nothing for my friends to form a line between here and Inaba. There are enough crocodiles to stretch from here even as far as China or India. Did you ever see so many crocodiles?"

Then the whole company of crocodiles arranged themselves in the water so as to form a bridge between the Island of Oki and the mainland of Inaba. When the hare saw the bridge of crocodiles, he said:

"How splendid! I did not believe this was possible. Now let me count you all! To do this, however, with your permission, I must walk over on your backs to the other side, so please be so good as not to move, or else I shall fall into the sea and be drowned!"

So the hare hopped off the island on to the strange bridge of crocodiles, counting as he jumped from one crocodile's back to the other:

"Please keep quite still, or I shall not be able to count. One, two, three, four, five, six, seven, eight, nine—"

Thus the cunning hare walked right across to the mainland of Inaba. Not content with getting his wish, he began to jeer at the crocodiles instead of thanking them, and said, as he leapt off the last one's back:

"Oh! you stupid crocodiles, now I have done with you!"

And he was just about to run away as fast as he could. But he did not escape so easily, for so soon as the crocodiles understood that this was a trick played upon them by the hare so as to enable him to cross the sea, and that the hare was now laughing at them for their stupidity, they became furiously angry and made up their minds to take revenge. So some of them ran after the hare and caught him. Then they all surrounded the poop little animal and pulled out all his fur. He cried out loudly and entreated them to spare him, but with each tuft of fur they pulled out they said:

"Serve you right!"

When the crocodiles had pulled out the last bit of fur, they threw the poor hare on the beach, and all swam away laughing at what they had done.

The hare was now in a pitiful plight, all his beautiful white fur had been pulled out, and his bare little body was quivering with pain and bleeding all over. He could hardly move, and all he could do was to lie on the beach quite helpless and weep over the misfortune that had befallen him. Notwithstanding that it was his own fault that had brought all this misery and suffering upon the white hare of Inaba, any one seeing the poor little creature could not help feeling sorry for him in his sad condition, for the crocodiles had been very cruel in their revenge.

Just at this time a number of men, who looked like King's sons, happened to pass by, and seeing the hare lying on the beach crying, stopped and asked what was the matter.

The hare lifted up his head from between his paws, and answered them, saying:

"I had a fight with some crocodiles, but I was beaten, and they pulled out all my fur and left me to suffer here—that is why I am crying."

Now one of these young men had a bad and spiteful disposition. But he feigned kindness, and said to the hare:

"I feel very sorry for you. If you will only try it, I know of a remedy which will cure your sore body. Go and bathe yourself in the sea, and then come and sit in the wind. This will make your fur grow again, and you will be just as you were before."

Then all the young men passed on. The hare was very pleased, thinking that he had found a cure. He went and bathed in the sea and then came out and sat where the wind could blow upon him.

But as the wind blew and dried him, his skin became drawn and hardened, and the salt increased the pain so much that he rolled on the sand in his agony and cried aloud.

Just then another King's son passed by, carrying a great bag on his back. He saw the hare, and stopped and asked why he was crying so loudly.

But the poor hare, remembering that he had been deceived by one very like the man who now spoke to him, did not answer, but continued to cry.

But this man had a kind heart, and looked at the hare very pityingly, and said:

"You poor thing! I see that your fur is all pulled out and that your skin is quite bare. Who can have treated you so cruelly?"

When the hare heard these kind words he felt very grateful to the man, and encouraged by his gentle manner the hare told him all that had befallen him. The little animal hid nothing from his friend, but told him frankly how he had played a trick on the crocodiles and how he had come across the bridge they had made, thinking that he wished to count their number: how he had jeered at them for their stupidity, and then how the crocodiles had revenged themselves on him. Then he went on to say how he had been deceived by a party of men who looked very like his kind friend: and the hare ended his long tale of woe by begging the man to give him some medicine that would cure him and make his fur grow again.

When the hare had finished his story, the man was full of pity towards him, and said:

"I am very sorry for all you have suffered, but remember, it was only the consequence of the deceit you practiced on the crocodiles."

"I know," answered the sorrowful hare, "but I have repented and made up my mind never to use deceit again, so I beg you to show me how I may cure my sore body and make the fur grow again."

"Then I will tell you of a good remedy," said the man. "First go and bathe well in that pond over there and try to wash all the salt from your body. Then pick some of those kaba flowers that are growing near the edge of the water, spread them on the ground and roll yourself on them. If you do this the pollen will cause your fur to grow again, and you will be quite well in a little while."

The hare was very glad to be told what to do, so kindly. He crawled to the pond pointed out to him, bathed well in it, and then picked the kaba flowers growing near the water, and rolled himself on them.

To his amazement, even while he was doing this, he saw his nice white fur growing again, the pain ceased, and he felt just as he had done before all his misfortunes.

The hare was overjoyed at his quick recovery, and went hopping joyfully towards the young man who had so helped him, and kneeling down at his feet, said:

"I cannot express my thanks for all you have done for me! It is my earnest wish to do something for you in return. Please tell me who you are?"

"I am no King's son as you think me. I am a fairy, and my name is Okuni-nushi-no-Mikoto," answered the man, "and those beings who passed here before me are my brothers. They have heard of a beautiful Princess called Yakami who lives in this province of Inaba, and they are on their way to find her and to ask her to marry one of them. But on this expedition I am only an attendant, so I am walking behind them with this great big bag on my back."

The hare humbled himself before this great fairy Okuni-nushi-no-Mikoto, whom many in that part of the land worshiped as a god.

"Oh, I did not know that you were Okuni-nushi-no-Mikoto. How kind you have been to me! It is impossible to believe that that unkind fellow who sent me to bathe in the sea is one of your brothers. I am quite sure that the Princess, whom your brothers have gone to seek, will refuse to be the bride of any of them, and will prefer you for your goodness of heart. I am quite sure that you will win her heart without intending to do so, and she will ask to be your bride."

Okuni-nushi-no-Mikoto took no notice of what the hare said, but bidding the little animal goodby, went on his way quickly and soon overtook his brothers. He found them just entering the Princess's gate.

Just as the hare had said, the Princess could not be persuaded to become the bride of any of the brothers, but when she looked at the kind brother's face she went straight up to him and said:

"To you I give myself," and so they were married.

This is the end of the story. Okuni-nushi-no-Mikoto is worshiped by the people in some parts of Japan, as a god, and the hare has become famous as "The White Hare of Inaba." But what became of the crocodiles nobody knows.

Yuki-onna (雪女, the snow woman) from the Hyakkai-Zukan (百怪図巻) 1737 Sawaki Suushi (佐脇嵩之)

http://www.trussel.com/hearn/yuki.htm

The Edo period and Japan's fables provide a model for a sustainable Japan

Yuki-onna by Lafcadio Hearn (Koizumi Yakumo)
from Kwaidan (1904)

In a village of Musashi Province, there lived two woodcutters: Mosaku and Minokichi. At the time of which I am speaking, Mosaku was an old man; and Minokichi, his apprentice, was a lad of eighteen years. Every day they went together to a forest situated about five miles from their village. On the way to that forest there is a wide river to cross; and there is a ferryboat. Several times a bridge was built where the ferry is; but the bridge was each time carried away by a flood. No common bridge can resist the current there when the river rises.

Mosaku and Minokichi were on their way home, one very cold evening, when a great snowstorm overtook them. They reached the ferry; and they found that the boatman had gone away, leaving his boat on the other side of the river. It was no day for swimming; and the woodcutters took shelter in the ferryman's hut, – thinking themselves lucky to find any shelter at all. There was no brazier in the hut, nor any place in which to make a fire: it was only a two-mat hut, with a single door, but no window. Mosaku and Minokichi fastened the door, and lay down to rest, with their straw rain-coats over them. At first they did not feel very cold; and they thought that the storm would soon be over.

The old man almost immediately fell asleep; but the boy, Minokichi, lay awake a long time, listening to the awful wind, and the continual slashing of the snow against the door. The river was roaring; and the hut swayed and creaked like a junk at sea. It was a terrible storm; and the air was every moment becoming colder; and Minokichi shivered under his raincoat. But at last, in spite of the cold, he too fell asleep.

He was awakened by a showering of snow in his face. The door of the hut had been forced open; and, by the snow-light (*yuki-akari*), he saw a woman in the room, – a woman all in white. She was bending above Mosaku, and blowing her breath upon him; – and her breath was like a bright white smoke. Almost in the same moment she turned to Minokichi, and stooped over him. He tried to cry out, but found that he could not utter any sound. The white woman bent down over him, lower and lower, until her face almost touched him; and he saw that she was very beautiful, – though her eyes made him afraid. For a little time she continued to look at him; – then she smiled, and she whispered: – "I intended to treat you like the other man. But I cannot help feeling some pity for you, – because you are so young.... You are a pretty boy, Minokichi; and I will not hurt you now. But, if you ever tell anybody – even your own mother about what you have seen this night, I shall know it; and then I will kill you.... Remember what I say!"

With these words, she turned from him, and passed through the doorway. Then he found himself able to move; and he sprang up, and looked out. But the woman was nowhere to be seen; and the snow was driving furiously into the hut. Minokichi closed the door, and secured it by fixing several billets of wood against it. He wondered if the wind had blown it open; – he thought that he might have been only dreaming, and might have mistaken the gleam of the snow-light in the doorway for the figure of a white woman: but he could not be sure. He called to Mosaku, and was frightened because the old man did not answer. He put out his hand in the dark, and touched Mosaku's face, and found that it was ice! Mosaku was stark and dead....

By dawn the storm was over; and when the ferryman returned to his station, a little after sunrise, he found Minokichi lying senseless beside the frozen body of Mosaku. Minokichi was promptly cared for, and soon came to himself; but he remained a long time ill from the effects of the cold of that terrible night. He had been greatly frightened also by the old man's death; but he said nothing about the vision of the woman in white. As soon as he got well again, he returned to his calling, going alone every morning to the forest, and coming back at nightfall with his bundles of wood, which his mother helped him to sell.

One evening, in the winter of the following year, as he was on his way home, he overtook a girl who happened to be traveling by the same road. She was a tall, slim girl, very good-looking; and she answered Minokichi's greeting in a voice as pleasant to the ear as the voice of a song-bird. Then he walked beside her; and they began to talk. The girl said that her name was O-Yuki; that she had lately lost both of her parents; and that she was going to Yedo, where she happened to have some poor relations, who might help her to find a situation as servant. Minokichi soon felt charmed by this strange girl; and the more that he looked at her, the handsomer she appeared to be. He asked her whether she was yet betrothed; and she answered, laughingly, that she was free. Then, in her turn, she asked Minokichi whether he was married, or pledged to marry; and he told her that, although he had only a widowed mother to support, the question of an "honorable daughter-in-law" had not yet been considered, as he was very young.... After these confidences, they walked on for a long while without speaking; but, as the proverb declares, *Ki ga aréba, mé mo kuchi hodo ni mono wo iu*: "When the wish is there, the eyes can say as much as the mouth." By the time they reached the village, they had become very much pleased with each other; and then Minokichi asked O-Yuki to rest awhile at his house. After some shy hesitation, she went there with him; and his mother made her welcome, and prepared a warm meal for her. O-Yuki behaved so nicely that Minokichi's mother took a sudden fancy to her, and persuaded her to delay her journey to Yedo. And the natural end of the matter was that Yuki never went to Yedo at all. She remained in the house, as an "honorable daughter-in-law."

O-Yuki proved a very good daughter-in-law. When Minokichi's mother came to die, — some five years later, — her last words were words of affection and praise for the wife of her son. And O-Yuki bore Minokichi ten children, boys and girls, — handsome children all of them, and very fair of skin.

The country-folk thought O-Yuki a wonderful person, by nature different from themselves. Most of the peasant-women age early; but O-Yuki, even after having become the mother of ten children, looked as young and fresh as on the day when she had first come to the village.

One night, after the children had gone to sleep, O-Yuki was sewing by the light of a paper lamp; and Minokichi, watching her, said: —

"To see you sewing there, with the light on your face, makes me think of a strange thing that happened when I was a lad of eighteen. I then saw somebody as beautiful and white as you are now – indeed, she was very like you." . . .

Without lifting her eyes from her work, O-Yuki responded: —

"Tell me about her.... Where did you see her?"

Then Minokichi told her about the terrible night in the ferryman's hut, – and about the White Woman that had stooped above him, smiling and whispering, – and about the silent death of old Mosaku. And he said: – "Asleep or awake, that was the only time that I saw a being as beautiful as you. Of course, she was not a human being; and I was afraid of her, – very much afraid, – but she was so white I . . . Indeed, I have never been sure whether it was a dream that I saw, or the Woman of the Snow." . . .

O-Yuki flung down her sewing, and arose, and bowed above Minokichi where he sat, and shrieked into his face: "It was I – I – I! Yuki it was! And I told you then that I would kill you if you ever said one word about it! . . . But for those children asleep there, I would kill you this moment! And now you had better take very, very good care of them; for if ever they have reason to complain of you, I will treat you as you deserve!" . . .

Even as she screamed, her voice became thin, like a crying of wind; – then she melted into a bright white mist that spired to the roof-beams, and shuddered away through the smoke-hole.... Never again was she seen.

Yuki-onna(雪女) from the Gazu Hyakki Yakō 1781